My Family, Leopards and My Litchi Tree

By Anjana Dutt

BLUEROSE PUBLISHERS
India | U.K.

Copyright © Anjana Dutt 2024

All rights reserved by author. No part of this publication may be reproduced, stored in a retrieval system or transmitted in any form or by any means, electronic, mechanical, photocopying, recording or otherwise, without the prior permission of the author. Although every precaution has been taken to verify the accuracy of the information contained herein, the publisher assumes no responsibility for any errors or omissions. No liability is assumed for damages that may result from the use of information contained within.

BlueRose Publishers takes no responsibility for any damages, losses, or liabilities that may arise from the use or misuse of the information, products, or services provided in this publication.

For permissions requests or inquiries regarding this publication, please contact:

BLUEROSE PUBLISHERS
www.BlueRoseONE.com
info@bluerosepublishers.com
+91 8882 898 898
+4407342408967

ISBN: 978-93-5989-182-8

Cover Design & Illustrations: Anjana Dutt
Typesetting: Rohit

First Edition: July 2024

These moments of my childhood in
Howrah, Calcutta, Ranchi, Hazaribagh and Dehradun,
remain in my mind as the highlights of my growing up years,
in the company of my grandparents, parents and my beloved older brother.
When life was lived at an easier pace, days and nights seemed endless,
full of promise and adventure.

*"To Dada, Aniruddha Das, my fellow adventurer
and my daughter Ayesha Dutt who keeps me young."*

Foreword

Anjana and I have known each other for forty years. Just out of college, we were colleagues in the Calcutta office of Ogilvy- the greatest advertising agency in the world. Anjana was a visualizer and I was a copywriter. I dare say I was a few years senior to her and earned a few hundred rupees more on the pay check. Anjana spent many decades in advertising honing her skills, mastering her craft. We have remained in infrequent touch in the last couple of decades. The WhatsApp from Anjana a few weeks ago read: "I have written a book about life in Calcutta and beyond. I am also illustrating it. I want you to write the foreword." Of course I said, yes. So here it is.

You have in your hand a beautifully illustrated book bursting with colour and memories. The pictures painted by Anjana's words are just as beguiling. They take us back to the scents and sounds of our childhood and all our collective adventures. We can lose ourselves in a riot of sensory stimulations, take a break from a long day at work, and come out at the other end calm, yet invigorated. This is a book transcending generations. This is a book a parent can read to a child. This is a book an older sibling can read to her younger sister or brother. This is a book a grandparent can read to a neighbour's grandchild. It takes us back to a time, not so long ago, which we have lost, but have not consciously recognised the loss. Or was it really a loss? Or did those times mould us to make us who we are today.

Titbits of history peppered into the narrative make this book special. The current GPO in Calcutta stands where the original Fort William was located and a brass strip embedded in the road marks the boundary of the original fort. This makes you want to reach the location and see if the strip is still there! Or in Mehrangarh Fort in Jodhpur, where fifteen sets of handprints of the wives and concubines of the Maharaja still stand witness of them committing Sati.

In this day of instant gratification and transient Instagram posts, this book is a reminder of the luxuries of lazy summer days, train journeys, badminton in the afternoons, trips to New Market and, of course, food. And more food.

Allow yourself to take in what you can see, hear, taste, touch and smell in the moment. Look up, down and sideways. Use all your senses including those you might sometimes ignore: the feel of the grass under foot, the greens of the palm trees, browns of the bark, the fragrance of the flowers, the beating of your hearts. The silence. The memory.

I invite you now to do the same with Anjana's book. A book that will make you pause for a moment to realise that our riches are not in the form of material things, but in ourselves. Our memories, our lives lived and handed down to the next generation as a precious gift. Anjana has done this so vividly and eloquently in her book, "My Family, Leopards & My Litchi Tree".

Derek O'Brien - Parliamentarian, author.

Introduction

If anyone asks me to define Time - I don't know, I've never measured it, but today I was reassured it existed in Anjana's memories, reviving my lost ones.

Similarity? Or was it the sameness of our era gone by? And the use of words long forgotten because of the misty passage of Time … her Dida (grandmother) separating vegetables and sharpening her *boti*: my Dida sitting on a *piri,* cooking on a clay oven while the *boti* lay on its side, usefulness over.

Are these my childhood memories or hers?

And Grundig? I bet our grandchildren won't know the name …my father gave me one with some 45s, Cliff Richard, the Kingston Trio, Bobby Darin and others.

Who hasn't read Hardy, Twain etc who hasn't heard of Salim Ali's "Book of Indian Birds" or gone for a joyful walk with one's father?

I love Calcutta.
With its crumbling grand colonial buildings.
I could never live anywhere else.

Where has Time taken away Dadu, Dida, Ma, my father, the *'Bharar Ghor'* with its goodies and intoxicating smells ….
Where is my beloved city?

Curl up with a steaming plate of *khichdi* and *begun bhaja* and open Anjana's "My Family, Leopards and My Litchi Tree" to rediscover your own childhood through these nostalgic and heartfelt stories, and her wonderfully apt illustrations, when life was lived within the security and companionship of family…

Moon Moon Sen Dev Varma

Contents

Ora toh Engleesh 1

Flowers, Flowers and More Flowers 3

Kutno, Chanel #5 and Sliding Bloomers 4

Uthon, Kolabagan and Bori 7

Bhandar Ghor, Meat-safes and Nimki 8

Dunlop Pillows, Sirens and Kashphool 11

Boulders, Leopards and Patishapta 12

Star Fruit, Pebbles and China Grass 14

Soot, Sunbirds and My Litchi Tree 16

First Day Covers, Onions and Grimacing Gargoyles 19

Snow White, Lava and Paper Boats 20

Robbers, Waterfalls and Wild Strawberries 22

Sidecars, Cows and Eucalyptus Trees 24

Badminton, Fossils and an Orangutan 26

Leather Suitcases, Books and Hair Pins 29

Fish, Flowers and Waxpol Polish 30

Grundig, Wynton Marsalis and a Shaky Old Building 33

Chameleons, Squirrels and Fantailed Pigeons 34

Ice packs, Bread Pudding and Sati 36

Sticky Blue Plumbago and a Furry White Tail 38

Bridges, Cows and Caramel Custard 40

Singer Sewing Machines, Buttons and a Purse... 41

Victoria Amazonica, Mad Trees and Sher Shah Suri 42

Double Cream, Kalimpong Cheese and Eggs... 45

Airguns, Tigers and Trapeze Artists 46

Backing Trams, Swinging Trees and an Orange Flame... 49

Kites, Rathmela and Pink Sugar Maths 51

The Riverside, Picnic Baskets and Warehouses 52

Reed Organs, Magh Utsav and the Indian Flag 55

Christmas Cake, Ham and a Tree 57

Teatime, Bottlebrush and a Cycle.. 58

Glossary... 61

Ora toh Engleesh

Childhood memories are wonderous. Things that fascinate us as kids often determine the paths we explore as adults, sometimes pointing the way to a chosen profession or career.

Multicolored caterpillars carefully housed in shoe boxes with breathing holes punched into them, grubby fingers placing crunchy green leaves for the creatures to chomp on as they morphed into moths and butterflies might lead a child to pursue the delights of entomology later in life.

In my case, though our garden offered many fascinating options such as birds, flowers, the occasional squeaky and somewhat terrifying moles, bees, haughty large black ants, with their quivering antennae and mud… squishy warm wet mud, my attention veered towards conquering the fear of a language that separated me from those mysterious ladies in veils and long blue gowns who ruled my school. The Irish nuns. They seemed quite otherworldly as they glided along the corridors on soft soled shoes, gowns floating in orderly pleats around their ankles, appearing suddenly when you were least expecting them.

At the age of four I was enrolled in the nursery class of St Thomas's School, just a kilometer away from the safety of home. With its tall black iron gates and handlebar mustachioed guard who swung it open on ominously screechy hinges, school was rather terrifying. Away from the cocooned safety of home, surrounded by unfamiliar adults and noisy children, I was for the most part a quiet observer, happy to maintain my silence and participate in conversations and group activities only when I had to. I was no introvert. On the contrary I was known to be a chatterbox at home with my cousins, but this was unfamiliar territory. The red building with its green shutters seemed ominously imposing to my four-year-old sensibilities. The long olive-green corridors, where if you dawdled a scowling nun would suddenly appear out of nowhere and prompt you to quicken your pace. At the same time, running down corridors was banned because we were supposed to be 'little ladies', not mannerless 'hooligans' who didn't know any better.

One morning I was dropped off to school by our trusty elderly driver (who we called Motor Babu) in our somewhat odd grey hot-cross-bun-shaped Austin Somerset (that was deemed perfect for us kids, since it was built like a tank). Motor Babu, an elderly tall man with a great big paunch and kindly smile, dressed in his signature light blue uniform, walked me to the gate and drove off with my older brother to St Xavier's School, far, far away in Calcutta. What he didn't realise was that the school had declared it a holiday for some odd reason, and students and their parents who had not received the news were being asked to go home.

Here begins my tale of woe. Faced with the scary school building and two intimidating nuns with their implacable faces,

I stood transfixed with horror. What on earth was I to do? No Motor Babu to take me back to the security of home. An eerily quiet school building, and just a few similarly stranded kids looking lost as the nuns herded them into an orderly line. The morning sun hurt my already weepy eyes and I hastily wiped them with the neat white hanky pinned to my tunic. I had no idea what I should do nor where I should go, as I haplessly gazed around the school yard.

Luckily, a friend of my parents, who had come to drop his daughter off, recognised me and offered to drop me home on his scooter. Imagine my trepidation, never having even seen a two-wheeler from close quarters, and now being expected to climb onto one, and not fall off once we took off. After several minutes spent assuring the nuns that I would be safely transported home, the nuns reluctantly let me join father and daughter and I clambered on to the rear seat, clutching on to my friend as we rode away towards home. The scooter bucked and pranced around potholes, and I narrowly escaped falling off and landing on the tarmac. I had never been as relieved to see our front gate with its cheery yellow wooden slats and I jumped off as soon as the scooter entered our driveway.

Off I went to relate my misadventures to my grandmother, who I knew would wipe away my tears with a warm hug and perhaps a *jeebeygoja* (sugar coated pastry) or two and a cool glass of lemonade. She consoled me as I knew she would, expressing horror at my predicament, promising that this sort of thing would never happen again...perhaps she feared that I may get permanently scarred and refuse to attend school in the future!

Later my grandpa (who took poor Motor Babu to task for abandoning me at the school gate) asked me "Why didn't you tell the nuns to telephone us, so I could have brought you home?" My answer caused much merriment for years to come, especially after I conquered my fear of the language and graduated with English Honours…I said with tears in my voice, *"Kintu ora to Engleesh"* (But, they are English!)

Flowers, Flowers and More Flowers

One of the many things I miss, is making garlands with *Shiuli* flowers picked from the tree in our Howrah garden. For some reason, the tree attracted caterpillars… the hairy spiky kind that hurt really bad if you accidentally touched one. Which reminds me of the time I sat on a ledge in the garden and got one embedded in my calf. The pain was excruciating. Liberal applications of vinegar and a tweezer finally got the spikes out but not before tears overtook me. The *Bel phool* bushes were reserved for Dida. Once the flowers bloomed a few were picked for her by the gardener and lovingly placed in a silver bowl with a little water by her. Another flower she liked to add to the bowl of Bel was *Jui* or Jasmine. A plant of jasmine was trained to grow over a trellis and its flowers rained down on me when I walked under it.

The red *Rangan* flower was a favourite, not so much for its beauty but because the blossom was filled with nectar one could easily extract by gently sucking the thin end. One had to be careful not to accidentally suck in the stamen. It was a delicacy the big ticklish black ants loved as well so it was prudent to brush them off before tasting!

Another floret which grew wild was the pretty yellow Rain flower. It's delicate crocus like blooms growing on grass-like bright green stems often appeared on the edges of the lawn and were treated like weeds that I happily picked for my tiny vases. At some time in the past a few seeds must have appeared in the garden and they grew in unexpected places.

Dida was fond of creating small landscapes in the square window boxes overlooking the lawn. With carefully arranged rocks and bonsai plants, tiny jade and cacti, she made each box unique and quite fascinating. They looked like hillsides with mossy paths, trees and rocky outcrops, with natural waterfalls when it rained. She added tiny ceramics houses to add that extra mystique to the mountains.

Summers meant dahlias and sleepy sunflowers that showed their bright faces when the sun shone on them. Plants were arranged in order of size to best show their flowers once they bloomed, so rows of the shorter chrysanthemum in a variety of colours were planted in front of the dahlias, tall tuberoses and gladioli. Petunias and pansies were planted in tubs to line the edges of the pink yellow and white path running alongside the garden, replaced by other seasonal flora in autumn.

Dida replenished her stock of seeds and seedlings with regular visits to Sutton Seeds and the Horticultural Gardens. Winter meant an outing to the annual flower show at the 'Horticulture' where we admired the rows upon rows of exotic plants and marveled at the ikebana arrangements. I learnt the basics of flower arranging from her and my Mom and was entrusted with the task of creating interesting displays at home. The New Market flower shops were a favourite stop and they vied for attention with their colourful displays. Pink and yellow roses, Queen Anne's Lace flowers and gladioli were often bought for arrangements at home.

Kutno, Chanel No. 5 and Sliding Bloomers

One 'ritual' I remember my Dida performing was the practice of slicing different vegetables in the morning to prepare for the various meals to follow, otherwise known as *kutno*. Every dish required a specific cut, and the ever-present *boti* (Bengali kitchen knife), sharpened regularly by the bicycle riding, travelling knife grinder found pride of place in the center of the *dalan or uthon* (courtyard) with brass *thalas* (plates) and *jhuris* (wicker baskets) containing vegetables, ranged around. Dida in her starched sari, sat on a raised *pidi* (low wooden stool), her bunch of keys tied to the end of her *anchal* (end of a sari), separating different vegetables for different curries and fries, for lunch, tea and dinner as her personal maid scurried about to do her bidding.

There were circular *chaklas* (discs) of *begun* (brinjals) for *bhajas* (fritters), finely sliced potatoes for *jhurjhure* (finely cut) fries, *haldi* (turmeric) and salt sprinkled *ucchey* (bitter gourd) and a bunch of stuff for *chorchori* (mixed vegetable curry), including bright orange pumpkin and fresh green leafy vegetables… all placed in receptacles of different sizes after being thoroughly washed in *gamlas*(basins) of potassium permanganate and then fresh water. Every dish required a specific cut of vegetable, every meal a combination of curries and fries.

I loved watching this daily ritual, marveling at her dexterity as she cut, sliced and diced each piece with care, all the while regaling me with stories of the past as I sat on a matching *pidi*, knees drawn, elbows resting on them, with my chin comfortably cushioned in my palms as I scooted into a comfortable position, drinking it all in. Sometimes she recounted tales of how a particular dish was created. At other times Dida shared stories of interesting meals she had had on her travels in exotic countries far away from the humdrum of home. Frog's legs and lobster Thermidor in France, batter covered fish and chips in London, raw fish delicately sliced and artfully dressed in Japan.

How Dida managed to remain perfectly coiffed with her bun intact, rosy cheeks aglow, faintly redolent of Chanel No. 5, I never understood but always appreciated. Regardless of the household duties she performed, she remained unflappable and poised, regal and unquestionably the empress of our home. She was my hero, the one person I desperately wanted to be.

After a childhood spent in Orissa where her father was stationed, she graduated from Ravenshaw School in Cuttack one of India's oldest schools, established in 1868. Later in life she became a Prison Visitor, providing guidelines on improvements to be made in Women's Jails. Dida was a force to be reckoned with.

My visits to Dida's inner sanctum – her bedroom, were special. The room itself, that was a mirror image of mine across the courtyard had tall windows with wooden shutters painted white. Between the shutters and the glass panes on the inside were pretty curtains, mostly in pastel shades and edged with lace. In the afternoon after Dida had rested and woke up for her tea, I would knock and enter; the room cool and faintly redolent of yellow *Champa* buds resting in a silver bowl.

Tea time over, she would rise from her easy chair and make her way across to her mirror fronted wardrobe to choose a sari for the evening. As soon as the doors opened, I was greeted by the faint, but distinctive aroma of Channel No 5, her signature perfume. Apart from the stacks of neatly arranged saris, she had a collection of hand embroidered shawls which she had designed and stitched herself. Some were for home, pale beige or light grey with elegant flowers edging the corners. Others for more festive occasions were in deeper colours. I remember a particularly beautiful black pashmina which she had embellished with tiny gold blossoms.

And her evening bags – not a single one would be out of place in the gloved hands of a Parisian lady. One covered in matte black beads, with just a hint of dazzle from its silver clasp. Another clutch clad in peacock blue raw silk, with a spray of diamante flowers. She had bags, saris and elegant slippers for every kind of event she may want to attend on the arm of my equally elegantly suited grandfather. They made a striking pair and must have caused many a stir. From cruises to Venice and Paris, to explorations that took them to the foot of Mount Vesuvius, and the Great Barrier Reef, they had travelled extensively across the globe fueling my own desire to see far off places.

Though her own stories enthralled me, Dida loved to hear about my day at Loreto House, my new school and I would regale her with all the tiniest details. Including the embarrassing story about the elastic holding up my much-hated bloomers snapping just after lunch break, forcing me to remain glued to my chair, so that my undergarment wouldn't go sliding down. Like a flower in full bloom, it opened out and threatened to escape down my legs. When my brother came to pick me up from kindergarten, seeing my teary red face, and realising what had befallen me, he helped me up by clutching on to my billowing bloomers at my waist from outside my school tunic. He walked me to the car, all the while making sure the offending thing didn't slip past my uniform as it was threatening to do. We made our way home, amid laughter and some tears as I described how ashamed I'd felt. Dida applauded Dada's quick and thoughtful response and called him to her room for a hug. Needless to say, that was the last I saw of my bloomers.

Dida was extremely creative, and encouraged me to pursue my interest in art and writing. She taught me the intricacies of embroidery and lace making, so that I would always have a soft white embroidered hanky with a lace trim in my pocket wherever I went. She set up a vocational school for ladies to learn stitching, tailoring and embroidery, at our ancestral home. She and my Dadu also founded a school named after my great grandmother, Tara Sundari, which today, is one of the leading schools in Howrah.

But I digress! *Kutno* was an integral part of my life. When I was responsible enough to not accidentally hurt myself, Dida bought me a small *boti* and taught me how to correctly position my fingers to avoid cutting them.

Uthon, Kolabagan and Bori

The *uthon* or courtyard between Dida (paternal grandma) & Dadu's (paternal grandpa) wing and ours, was the center of activity for both houses. Hot summer days meant Dida would grind all kinds of Dal (lentil) and spices and add enough water to the various mixtures to make a paste. Large pieces of muslin would be washed and stretched out on U shaped *kulos* (wicker trays) and round bamboo trays and Dida would put dollops of the lentil mixtures on the muslin to create *boris* (sundried lentil dumplings) of different flavors and sizes. These would be dried on the *uthon* before being stored in glass jars. To prevent curious squirrels and marauding birds from sampling the delicacies, she kept them covered with wire mesh baskets.

Before storing or grinding spices and whole red chilies, they would be laid out to cure in the sun along with jackfruit seeds which were really tasty when added to curries. The spices and chilies would then be stored in large ceramic or glass jars and put away in the *bhandar ghor* (store room for household items), the repository of all things tasty.

My mom on the other hand liked making chutneys and achaars that she had learnt from her mother in Dehradun. There was one particular mango chutney we loved which made its annual appearance on the *uthon* in glass jars. It was made with finely cut pieces of mango, sugar, *panchphoron* (5 spices) and ginger. Mountains of mangoes were cut and mixed with the other ingredients and poured into glass jars, sealed and set out to cure in the sun.

The other favourite was the Pachranga Achaar which had its roots in North India. Chopped up pieces of mangoes, carrots, cauliflowers, round green ball like vegetables called *tenti*, and loads of spices like fenugreek, Nigella Seeds, mustard, fennel, chilies were mixed with mustard oil and poured into glass jars, and sunned for days in the courtyard.

Dida was a keen gardener and though her favourite was the garden in front, the kitchen garden behind our houses got a lot of attention from her too. She had planted a row of banana trees on one side and tall supari (beetle nut) trees lined the back wall along with coconut palms. There were two trees that gave us lots of lemons, one being a *gandharaj lebu* (aromatic lemon) tree with the most delightful aroma. Even the leaves crushed in your hand had the lovely tangy smell of the fruit.

There were plots for carrots, radish, and beans and a trellis for pumpkins and another for *karelas* (bitter gourd). She grew some herbs too and a curry leaf bush vied for attention with a hibiscus bush that had found its way to the back garden that no one had the heart to banish! There were two guava trees as well. Once in a while a banana tree would be chopped down and the *thor* (heart of a banana tree trunk) would be turned into a delicious curry. The flower too, *mocha* would be taken down once it was large enough, and after liberally coating her fingers with mustard oil, Dida would start the painstaking task of peeling back the petals to expose and remove the stamen and other inedible bits inside. Preparing *thor* and *mocha* were both rather time consuming so one knew better than to expect either on the menu too often! But with liberal amounts of grated coconut on top, they were both very tasty.

Bhandar Ghor, Meat-safes and Nimki

The concept of the *bhandar ghor* (store room for household items) has all but vanished from most homes, where space is at a premium and the refrigerator and kitchen cabinets have taken over the task of storing foodstuff. At home, even though there was a massive Fridge with a huge metal handle as elaborate as the ones on our wooden doors, some things could not be stored in its cool depths.

Like those crisp deep fried *kalojeerey* (black cumin) sprinkled little bite sized *nimkis* (savory snacks) packed in airtight biscuit tins with images of shepherdesses and sheep gamboling around their middle. Or the scrumptious *jeebeygoja* (sugar coated pastry) rimmed with crystallized sugar that begged to be eaten but were rationed and only appeared one at a time! How we loved them! The crunch of the first bite, the slightly softer inner folds and the pure sugar rush once it was eaten! These were stored in tightly shut biscuit tins to keep ants, moisture and our every ready fingers away.

And as a special treat there were glass jars of bouncy pink marshmallows dusted with powdered sugar that coated most of our faces when we'd eat them. Red and white twisted candy canes made their appearance in winter, along with individually wrapped lollipops and light green soft-centered mints.

All these treats were kept out of reach in tightly closed jars and tins in the 'meat-safe' This short wooden cupboard had a shiny brass lock shaped like a tiger eating its own tail. And this repository of yummies was kept in a cool corner of the *bhandar ghor* (larder sounds too Engleesh). The meat-safe had a fine metallic mesh for doors and windows, keeping the treats tantalisingly visible but unapproachable. It's four stumpy legs rested on wooden bowls filled with water, one under each foot. The level of the water had to be kept just right to create a moat to deter ants and other sweet seeking insects. Before refrigerators were invented, these meat-safes were used to store meat, butter, cheeses and other perishable food, though I don't know how long they stayed fresh enough to eat.

The *bhandar ghor* itself had tall green shutters kept closed to keep the sun and dust out. Its interior resembled a cool dark cave with huge metallic containers full of rice, various kinds of dal, flour and atta and ceramic mason jars or *boams* filled with sugar, salt and preserves lurking in corners or on the built-in cemented shelves. Home-made *panchrang achaar* (five spice pickle), *kuler achaar* (Indian plum pickle), and other delights were stored in clear glass containers, sealed shut to keep the damp air out.

The 'fridge' on the other hand was more easily breached! Home-made guava jellies, jams and the sticky dark chewy guava cheese which my maternal grandmother sent from Dehradun, rubbed shoulders with store bought strawberry jam and marmalade, rounds of soft smoked Bandel Cheese, round waxed buttery yellow cooking cheese from Kalimpong and *aamsatta* bricks (layers of sundried sweet mango pulp) clad in cellophane. Fresh brown eggs marched in neat rows in niches in the door, alongside pots of mustard and bottles of bright red tomato ketchup. Ice cream sodas bumped against ginger ale and water. But… the fridge had a tell-tale squeaky door and the moment it opened, and the inner light switched on, a frowning adult with arms on hips would materialise, so we'd retreat with bottles of cold water and sheepish grins.

For my 8th birthday, Ma had baked her famous chocolate cake with smooth chocolate butter icing between layers of moist cake and shiny glazed icing on the outside. She had also made large tubs of vanilla ice cream and both desserts were kept in the fridge to cool down for the teatime party. At noon, when she decided to check on them, we discovered to our horror that the fridge handle was stuck and no amount of pulling or persuasion worked, to open the door. Faced with a birthday party and no cake, Ma hurriedly baked a second simpler sponge cake with lemon icing. At 4 o'clock after everyone arrived and the party was well under way, the fridge door miraculously opened. We were delighted with the turn of events as we happily tucked into bowls of ice cream and two kinds of cake!

High tech refrigerators (sometimes talking with American accents) that spew out perfectly formed ice cubes and cold water from niches nestled on its sides are no match for the lure of the *bhandar ghor*. There is no romance in opening a silent door to pull out a tetra packed drink or sliced cheese. The smell and atmosphere of our *bhandar ghor* was far more enticing.

This store room or larder also served as a hideout during games of hide and seek, though the fear of mice and other things that scamper or crawl kept me out of its far corners. The tall wooden doors to this cave would be opened ceremoniously every morning for the day's rations to be measured out, and closed after dinner was done. The keys to this room, one of many that my Dida had on her key ring, were attached to the end of her *anchal* (end of a sari) for safekeeping.

Dunlop Pillows, Sirens and 'Kashphool'

I wonder if anyone else remembers the sirens of 1971 during the Bangladesh War? I seem to recall that we would pretend that we were being attacked by a flying squadron of enemy planes and my brother and I would hunker down under the staircase which seemed to be the safest place in the house. We wouldn't emerge until the All-Clear siren went off, and would listen to the radio for updates on the war.

The nine o'clock siren was another regular feature of our lives. Clocks and watches would be checked to the sound of the siren, to make sure they were running on time. Some factories also used sirens to announce their shift changes, with short blasts announcing accidents or trouble of some kind. The other memorable sound was the celebratory hoots of ships in the river, at the stroke of midnight on New Year's Eve, marking the passing of a year.

Sometimes, mostly at night when all was quiet, when we'd hear the long and short warning hoots of train horns, it would give rise to a feeling of dread… they were blown in a certain pattern to announce railway accidents. Living in close auditory proximity to the Howrah station and its accompanying yard, trains were an integral part of our lives.

Train journeys were the best way to travel. Car trips were fun too but sitting still for hours even when the places we drove through were picturesque, took a toll on my patience. The whole experience of train trips, with the planning of packed food to snack on, special long- lasting dinners to dine on, the AH Wheeler Book shop we invariably bought books for the journey, tossing a coin to decide who would sleep on the upper bunks… all added to the excitement of travelling by the railways. The hold-all would be packed with inflatable Dunlop pillows with their strange rubbery smell, only somewhat alleviated by the crisp cotton covers. Even though first-class cabins were given bed linen, we carried our own, believing (Dida and Ma) that it was more hygienic to do so. Unbreakable plates and glasses, insulated water bottles, a large picnic basket filled with edibles, and lots of board games made for thoroughly enjoyable trips.

For some reason, we felt the onset of hunger the minute the train would shudder and take off from the station! I loved the regular rhythm of the locomotive and though it made standing somewhat perilous when it picked up speed, the swaying motion made for a good night's sleep. Bagging the window while awake meant one could gaze out at the passing scenery, the bright green fields stretching for miles occasionally broken by clumps of trees and huts marking the presence of villages.

Village platforms with their cement benches, and lone ticket counters seemed full of untold stories of families waiting to greet visiting relatives from the city who may have migrated to pursue their dreams but still had ties to home. Unshed tears of new brides leaving their homes for places and lives unknown, filled with trepidation and a small measure of excitement at what lay ahead. I loved looking out for *Kashphool* (wild grass) along the tracks. Their feathery fronds and jaunty swaying made me think they were waving us along on our upcoming adventures.

Boulders, Leopards and Patishapta

My Pishima (father's sister) has a house in Hazaribagh just below the Canary Hill Reserve Forest. It's a lovely sprawling bungalow with a large garden which had an interesting feature. A pile of huge boulders that had probably rolled downhill from some rocky ledge and settled on the lawn.

There were three fairly large black boulders smoothened over time which I loved climbing on to sit at the very top. Behind the house, just a few yards away we could see the boundary line of the reserve forest, its dense thickness making it fairly difficult to see beyond the first line of trees.

One winter afternoon Pishima and I, the only two people at the house, decided to make *patishaptas* (sweet crepes) for tea time. I must have been around 12 years old, old enough to offer my services and was put to task, to sift the dry ingredients after measuring them out. Ground rice, flour and baking soda. Fairly soon I was liberally covered with flour, much to Pishima's amusement, (I could see her smile into her *anchal* when she thought I wasn't looking) but I carried on regardless, enjoying the mess I was making. The mixture of the dry stuff with milk and water, and the filling of shredded coconut and kheer were ready, and kept aside for the former to rest and the latter to cool down.

Thinking that I needed a break, Pishima sent me off to wash my face and run around in the garden. It was a lovely sunny day. The wind was cold and crisp, the sun a welcome warmth, flowers bloomed in orderly rows but… it was strangely silent. Wondering where the usually cacophonous birds had gone, I decided to sketch and brought out my trusty sketchbook and pencils, and headed for the boulders. The flat top of the highest one made it an ideal perch.

I suddenly heard Pishima's voice in a loud whisper, asking me to rush indoors. She kept saying, "taratari bhetorey esho" (get indoors now!) I turned tail and ran, instinctively slamming the front door behind me and I skidded to a stop in the kitchen where Pishima was looking out the window. She pointed and I looked! What a beautiful sight! Frightening but beautiful.

In the golden winter sunlight stretched out on the boulder I was heading towards; a young magnificent leopardess and 2 cubs were sunning themselves. The mother, though she looked relaxed, had her eyes open and alert for any signs of danger. We looked at them with awe and relief that we were safely inside. The gardener told us later that this family of three often sunbathed at that spot. Residents of the reserve forest, they were unaware that they were meant to stay inside its boundaries, wandering freely in the garden. The cubs played on the rocks as their mother kept a watchful eye on them, making sure they did not stray too far.

I learnt later that night that Pishima had once rescued a tiger cub that had lost its mother to a poacher and she hand fed it and raised it to a point where it could be reintroduced to the wild, giving him up reluctantly as he grew bigger. She had grown very attached to the cub but obviously could not keep him at her home in the middle of the city, in Ballygunge, in Calcutta.

Star fruit, Pebbles and China Grass

My paternal grandparents, Dadu and Dida, had a house in Ranchi. Being closer to Calcutta than Doon where my other set of grandparents lived, we would visit Ranchi often, for short breaks, mostly driving down for a few fun filled days.

They migrated to Ranchi through the warmer months, returning to Calcutta when it got too cold to stay on. Their trips were epic. For days prior to their journey the house would be in a state of excitement and controlled turmoil. Dida was highly organised, but it was still a bit chaotic, with suitcases and hold-alls being brought out of storage, large tiffin carriers and water jugs being scrubbed and sun dried for the journey.

The menu for meals on the train would be meticulously planned and, depending on the season, would consist of various kinds of food that would not perish on the way. Though it was an overnight journey, around eight or nine hours from Howrah, preparations had to be made for all meals. Evening tea , dinner at night and a light breakfast. As they aged, Dadu and Dida became less experimental about the food they ate, and were not fans of the railway canteen fare nor did they take chances with meals prepared on platforms, however delicious.

Packing for a few months in Ranchi would take time. Clothes, books, some linen, hobby items like knitting wool and needles, crochet sets, embroidery threads and needles and the wooden rings to stretch material over, would all be packed in trunks, hold-alls and leather valises. Freshly ground-spices would be packed in jars. Dida's makeup and personal care items would be placed in her leather case which was a squarish vanity box with a handle, in a beautiful ivory colour with shiny brass latches which had trays, pockets, secret compartments and a mirror inside the lid. The silver backed brush and combs, her wavy hair pins to secure her bun, her perfumed handkerchiefs, along with her creams and lotions went into specific pockets and her Chanel # 5 bottle in its white box was carefully placed inside.

My Dida's personal help, Ushadidi, would be outfitted for the stay with new clothes and a light shawl for the evenings. The driver was given a smart jacket, to keep out the Ranchi chill for the latter part of their stay. The Rover would leave a day early for Ranchi with Dida's personal assistant and the chauffeur. The car was packed with non-perishable food for the first few days in Ranchi. After reaching the house, with the help of the resident caretaker who lived on the premises with his family, doors and windows would be opened to air out the house and the rooms would be swept and dusted for my grandparent's arrival.

The Chauffer was given a shopping list by Dida, for fresh vegetables, chicken and eggs which he would buy from the local market in Ranchi. The following morning, he would collect my grandparents from Ranchi station and drive down to

Morabadi, to their estate. A pot of freshly brewed tea and breakfast would be laid out for their arrival on the covered veranda overlooking the garden.

Dida, a keen gardener, had overseen the planting of the orchard at the back of the property and the flower garden in front with the Christmas tree in the center of the oval lawn. This tree had grown tall with an odd posture, leaning towards the iron gates in front as though in greeting. The boundaries of the property on the two sides were created with a line of sandalwood bushes on the right and evergreen shrubs on the left. A huge Mohua tree stood to the left of the wrought iron gate and a *Gulmohar* on the other side. The driveway was lined with white oval pebbles that made cycling rather perilous (as I discovered after skidding headlong into a cactus plant and getting my knees embedded with thorns!) though approaching cars would announce their arrival with a musical crunching sound.

The single-story house looked like a chalet with a sloping red tiled roof and window boxes filled with flowers. The covered veranda on one side with its comfortable upholstered cane chairs and oval glass topped table was the best place for tea, to play board games, read or simply daydream.

What I remember about the orchard is the line of *'kamranga'* or star fruit trees. The semi ripe green fruit was very, very sour but sliced finely and sprinkled with a liberal coating of rock salt, though it set my teeth on edge, was lip-pursing good. The ripe yellow ones were sweeter but not as tasty. There were guavas and mangoes aplenty and *'tapari'* or cape gooseberry bushes. The kitchen garden grew carrots and green beans which tasted fresh and crunchy straight off the plants. I loved digging out the bright orange carrots, dusting off the soil before giving them a quick scrub under the garden tap and biting into them. Ruby red tomatoes, glowing amidst the somewhat hairy green leaves added sweetness to our salads. We were warned off the deeper end of the orchard where the undergrowth being thicker may have housed a critter or two.

One of the staple desserts my Dida made in Ranchi, was 'China grass' pudding. I have not tasted it anywhere else other than at her dining table. Its wobbly form and mild taste was quite unique and it's only recently that I discovered that it was made with *agar-agar*. Another thing we looked forward to was the occasional breakfast of hot freshly made *luchis* (fried flatbread) and *aloo dum* (potato curry), with a big fluffy omelet on the side. Dida would sometimes order duck's eggs for us, which tasted rich and a little gamey. Deep fried golden brown, orange yolks brimming with flavor, Dida would conjure up *dimer dalna* or egg curry with those tasty eggs and serve them with fresh parathas at dinnertime. At Dida's table we would wait for her to silently mouth grace before we began eating. Though she never insisted we say grace ourselves, she appreciated our silence and patience while she prayed.

Soot, Sunbirds and My Litchi Tree

Winter and spring vacations in Dehradun where our maternal grandparents had retired to, were filled with outdoor activities, the adventures starting at Howrah Station. Loud voices, the tinny station announcements and excited chatter from travelers going to far off places filled the air. The aromas of food and smoke swirled around us. After surrendering our luggage to two burly coolies in their red and dark blue uniforms and making sure that they were following us to the designated platform we would look eagerly for our bogie and jump aboard the Doon Express. It was a heady respite from the jostling busy platforms filled with passengers, vendors and coolies poshing iron carts filled to the brim with cargo. If you weren't careful to jump out of the way your toes could easily be run over by these overladen wagons.

Out came our story books, drawing books and crayons as we settled in to our compartment. The peculiar sooty smell of the train, the sticky blue rexine seats, the wobbly folding table that would serve as our dinner table and the place to play games were all familiar and spelt the start of a grand holiday. I loved sleeping on trains. From laying out the bedding to blowing up the air pillows and settling down with a book, I loved moving with the sway of the train and listening to the rhythm and sound of the wheels as they transported us to our destination over bridges and rivers and through tunnels. The two-day journey with stops at major stations to pick up meals, the call of vendors as we slowed down and stopped long enough to hop off and replenish our bottles and collection of snacks passed in a blur of excitement, till we reached Doon and alighted.

Sometimes my maternal grandpa would come to pick us up in his shiny black vintage Austin but that meant we would have to push it to start! It was extremely temperamental but no one was allowed to criticise it! At other times it was off to the *tonga* (horse carriage) stand with the smelly horses stamping their hooves with impatience, ready to trot off with or without passengers. Passing through the street markets below the clock tower or '*Ghanta Ghar*' as we perched on pieces of luggage, we'd make our way to Dalanwala by the banks of the river, ready to run around the garden and shake off the effects of the journey.

My Didama (maternal grandma) was a keen maker of jams and jellies, bottling seasonal fruits from the garden in delicious preserves. Plums, peaches, guava, mangoes, litchis… the list was endless, as was our appetite for hot buttered toast and a thick layer of fresh cream with jam. Nothing can beat the taste of that combination. We would bite into slices of sweetish milk bread with the glistening red spoonful of wobbly bright red jam on thick layers of cream, dollops of which would occasionally spill on to our plates if we were in a hurry.

Didama was a good cook, and spent quite a bit of time conjuring up delicious meals with a North Indian touch having lived in that part of the country after she got married, but she was equally interested in reading. Afternoons would find us lying down next to her in the huge canopied bed that needed a couple of wooden steps to climb on to, as she read us stories first from children's books and later as we reached our teens, short stories written by the great Bengali writers... such as Rabindranath Tagore, Sarat Chandra Chattopadhyay,, Bankim Chandra Chattopadhyay and others. We listened with rapt attention as the afternoons segued into the early evening and it was time for tea and snacks.

Her room was lined with glass fronted book cases filled with not just Bengali literature, but the classics as well, and we had our pick of Dickens, Thomas Hardy and other Victorian writers rubbing shoulders with Durrell and Mark Twain. I remember a particularly fascinating Bible, with beautiful illustrations, the pages separated with translucent paper to preserve the drawings. I poured over this huge book, carefully turning the pages as I marveled at the jewel like colours and golden highlights, each chapter beginning with an elaborate calligraphic drop letter.

We were encouraged to spend time outdoors to drink in the fresh air and I loved climbing trees, spending many happy hours sitting on a particular horizontal branch of a litchi tree next to the portico. There, story book or drawing book in hand I'd pretend as a child, to be on a horse or a boat depending on what I was reading at the time. Summers in Doon meant I could eat fresh fruit off the tree, though I'd often have to brush off ants and other insects who vied for the same delicacy.

Once, while I was perched up 'my' tree, a shiny-black Ambassador drove onto the graveled driveway and a smart uniformed driver leapt out to open the rear door for a somewhat grim looking elderly gentleman in a suit. He jumped when I, spying him from my perch, demanded to know his identity. Breaking into a smile he said, "I'm your Dadu (Grandfather)" to which I indignantly replied with "No you're not! You are lying. Wait here while I call my real Dadu". Clambering down the tree I rushed indoors to my grandfather and indignantly related the conversation. He looked horrified and ran outside muttering "He must be so angry. Must have left for Delhi by now." Far from looking annoyed the gentleman outside was grinning, as he greeted Dadu and said, "Your granddaughter is absolutely right! You are her real Dadu. I'm just your older brother, who is also her Dadu, but she didn't know that. No one in our family has ever dared speak to me this way. You must be so proud of her – I certainly am!".

Apparently, this gentleman had a legendary temper, but my fearless demand for honesty had not just surprised him, he thoroughly approved of it. This became an oft repeated story and was embellished by him at every family gathering much to my embarrassment.

My brother and I were devoted bird watchers and armed with Salim Ali's 'The Book of Indian Birds', we built ourselves an 'observation post' camouflaged with twigs and leaves and set up a bird bath to attract them, scattering seeds on its rim. From exotic long-forked-tailed black and white Flycatchers to the brilliant red Sun birds and other colourful species, many afternoons were spent crouched in wait for these feathery visitors. The shiny black raucous Ravens paid us many visits, loudly announcing their noisy presence. We would read up on the habits and natural habitats of the ones we spied, sometimes using our binoculars on birds that alighted further away, diligently making notes in our special journal.

First Day Covers, Onions and Grimacing Gargoyles

Sundays were kept for hobbies and adventures. Dada, and I were members of the Philatelic Club, ardent collectors of stamps and first day covers. The moment we heard of a new issue we would drive down to the GPO and head for the Philatelic Bureau where our favourite stamp issuing officer sat, and wait our turn to get our first day covers.

The GPO building is one of Calcutta's iconic buildings not just because it's a remnant of the Raj but because of the history surrounding it. The site where the GPO is located now was actually the site of the first Fort William. Its construction began around 1696, and continued through 1706. The original fort housed, among other things, the East India Company's factory, the Governor's mansion, living quarters for the employees of the factories of the company, and various offices and godowns. When the new Nawab of Bengal, Siraj-ud-Daula attacked Calcutta in 1756, the fort fell. St. Anne's Church, Calcutta's first Church, which stood where the main rotunda of the Writers' Building stands today, was also destroyed in the attack. The heavily damaged fort was ultimately torn down, and the GPO and other buildings took its place.

An alley beside the post office was the site of the guardhouse that housed the infamous 1756 Black Hole of Calcutta. The current GPO was designed in 1864 by Walter B. Grenville, consulting architect to the government of India from 1863 to 1868. The staircase at the eastern side of the GPO has a brass plate, marking the eastern end of the Old Fort William. There used to be a brass strip embedded in the road, marking the boundary of the original Fort William as well as a barely visible strip running down the staircase of the GPO. Stepping gingerly while balancing on that strip was a ritual we had mastered to perfection, daring one another to not fall off the narrow shiny piece of history on to the tarred dark present.

We liked exploring old buildings and historical sites, stopping to take photographs of interesting wrought iron railings on crumbling balconies that looked too fragile to support their weight. North of the Howrah Bridge was full of *Rajbaris* (royal mansions) and narrow streets, where one often came across plaques that once proudly announced in fancy calligraphy the titled owner's names of one-time grand structures now fallen on hard times. There were traces in unexpected places of faded opulence and zamindari excesses. A brilliant stained-glass fanlight above a weathered door here, a dusty cobwebbed chandelier there, gargoyles leering at passers-by, forlorn stone fairies dancing on parapets supporting clothes lines with wet sarees drying in the hot summer sun.

We loved exploring the old Silver Mint on Strand Road. Its towering pillars and sweeping staircase resounding with the footsteps of busy merchants long gone fascinated us. I imagined top hatted, black coated, cane carrying British East India Company men going about their businesses there. Getting to it meant navigating the slippery cobblestones of *'Posta'* the heart of wholesale Calcutta where potato and onion laden lorries would lurch from puddle to puddle, threatening to keel over and spill their slippery load. Sometimes we got stuck behind one of those behemoths and I imagined getting buried under mounds of smelly onions!

Snow White, Lava and Paper Boats

I spent a lot of time with my Dida and a favourite part of my day was to visit her in the evening when she'd get ready for company. She had a separate dressing room with two massive mirrored wardrobes shining with beeswax and an elaborate dressing table with 3 mirrors that could swivel, with an assortment of exotic perfumes, silver backed brushes and a comb and a silver backed mirror for close up inspections of her hair arranged neatly on top. Creams, lotions and face powders in pretty flowered containers sat on lace doilies next to an oval silver plate with her hair pins.

I never saw her with her hair undone outside this inner sanctum where she could be her natural self away from scrutiny. Being married to the eldest son she was the head of the family and I guess she felt compelled to appear dignified and well turned out at all times. To me as a kid, she was simply my Dida who never had a hair out of place or a crumpled pleat to her sari. She was perfect!

My love for perfumes is definitely inherited from her. Her room always had a faint aroma of Chanel No 5, her favourite. Sometimes she'd allow me to choose her sari for the evening and the matching handbag. Silver sequined evening purses nestled next to black velvet ones with elaborate silver clasps, pride of place being given to one particular beaded purse covered in tiny lapis beads that she had brought back from Egypt.

Dida was fond of making dolls out of unusual material. There was a large glass showcase with Snow White and her 7 Dwarfs made from different items. The heads were all made of eggshells with the faces painted on, the bodies were created with cotton-stuffed pieces of skin colored material and the clothes meticulously stitched with buttons and bows and bits of embroidery and lace. Their hair was created from wool and Snow White had on a blue bonnet to match her blue dress. The whole display was beautiful with the 8 dolls standing on a base of green velvet that looked like grass in a meadow.

Just outside the living room, next to the glass case with Snow White inside, at the base of the staircase leading to the second floor was Dadu's Grandfather clock. He would wind it with a brass key that hung inside the case. The clock was 6 feet tall and had a shiny brass pendulum and it chimed every hour to announce the time. I used to sit on the bottom stair and stare at its steady movement, mesmerised by its precise swing from side to side. The clock face had an elaborate pair of hands in black and golden Roman numerals on a glossy cream base. The body of the clock was made of reddish-brown polished wood and to my diminutive height, soared way up towards the ceiling.

Dida had travelled the world by the time I came around and every memento in her living room glass cabinet had a story to relate…a piece of coral from the Great Barrier Reef (illegal today), a clump of lava from Vesuvius which ate through the little silver plate it sat on. Paper and cloth hand painted dolls from Japan vied for attention with Venetian glass necklaces. Apart from the mini Eiffel Tower and Beefeater hat wearing Queens Guard soldier there were porcelain shepherdesses, Delft blue houses and a windmill, a tiny exquisite silver purse fashioned out of fine silver wire, a pair of wooden clogs, delicate glass birds with colourful wings, a miniature tea set, Japanese fans with elaborate designs painted on them, a Japanese doll made of thick paper in a red velvet kimono, and a mini Chinese folding screen with a black and white bamboo design painted on rice paper framed in black wood that stood in a corner.

Every few months we would carefully remove all the mementos shelf by shelf, and clean the inside before dusting and polishing the pieces and putting them back in their designated places. Dida had entrusted me with dusting the shelves and cleaning the glass panes with damp newspaper balls while she sat on a matching mora and directed me. It was a job I cherished because I got to ask her about each piece before they were put back in place. I never tired of hearing their tales. But the best stories were those of her adventures as a child.

She grew up in Cuttack. Her parents obviously were well established socially judging by her stories of road trips and holidays to far off places. I loved the one about the reserve forest. They were travelling through a densely forested part of the Chotanagpur plateau in their car. Packed along with their overnight gear were two rifles to be brought out in case they met up with any wild animals. The car had running boards where two of the house boys were stationed as lookouts. Quite the safari in my eyes. As evening approached, the 2 lamps on the sides were lit to penetrate the deepening shadows. The kids in the back fell silent, as they dozed off and the forest sounds grew louder. The ever-present crickets, birds returning to their nests, nocturnal animals waking up for their nightly foraging in the undergrowth.

Suddenly a deep growl from the bushes stunned everyone into silence. A pair of eyes glowing malevolently looked back at them followed by another growl. The two lookouts who had been instructed to jump into the car should they encounter any animals forgot their orders and ran into the night! Their piercing screams shattered the quiet and the growling animal decided prudence was better than bravery and fled into the forest!

My great grandfather lit his trusty stainless-steel torch and chased after the boys, bringing them back to the car, and the remaining journey was filled with an equal measure of merriment at their cowardice and that of the four-legged beast they had scared off with their screams. This story was told and retold many times with embellishments added on at each telling.

Rainy afternoons were the best. Dida would lie back in her easy chair with the long wooden arm rests while I sat curled up on her bed with a warm shawl to keep out the chill as I listened to her stories. Sudden squalls in the summer would find us making paper boats to float in the rising water on the *uthon*. Dida taught us the art of making paper boats and my brother and I would have boat races which would last only as long as the boats remained afloat. Rainy days also meant warm khichuri with *kurkurey aloo bhaja*, (potato crisps) a shiny full boiled egg for us kids and thick creamy *mishti doi* (sweet yogurt) to follow. Life was good!

Robbers, Waterfalls and Wild Strawberries

Dehradun or Doon with its wonderful greenery, endless forested hillsides and the chill in the air that we enjoyed breathing out in puffy, cloudy breaths, had so many interesting spots to wander in.

The dry river bed near the house was a fascinating place because of the wealth of pebbles and occasional fossils we found there. With the *titir* birds flying overhead and the sun warming our hands and faces, many hours were spent wandering around collecting souvenirs. If we were lucky, we'd come across wild strawberries. Tiny jewel like fruits hid within the scrawny bushes, some sweet some sour and unripe but delicious nonetheless.

Up river, a favourite place we often visited was a particular tunnel called the Robber's Cave locally known as '*Gucchu Pani*', both eerie and fascinating. Legend has it that robbers and highway men would hide their plunder in some of the many stone caves within the 500- or 600-meter tunnel carved out by the river as it flowed down the mountain. As you entered, the stone walls on either side looked like two craggy ominous faces glaring at one another.

It is believed that this was where Dronacharya, the Guru and educator of the Pandavas and Kauravas from the Mahabharata, lived with his son Ashwatthama. When the water level in the stream went down in winter to ankle-deep depths, we could walk quite a long way in, marveling at the stone formations. At some point in the distant past, landslides or erosion had caused the roof to collapse allowing the natural light to peep through, to illuminate our journey. There were deep shelves on both sides, and niches where one could easily imagine thieves hiding gold and caskets of ill begotten riches. Keeping a lookout for long forgotten loot, hoping to discover treasure chests bound in brass, we would clutch hands and wade through the semi darkness, hoping we wouldn't encounter any bandana sporting robbers brandishing daggers, inside. The cave opened out into a waterfall at the end of the tunnel that tumbled down the mountainside, filling the air with a fine spray.

There were two waterfalls amongst the many that we visited often. Sansan Dhara (which was more of a trickle with a pool underneath) and Sahasradhara which was thrilling. The journey to the falls around and over the forested hills was lovely in itself. Getting sprayed by the falling water, wading at the bottom of the falls and eventually getting soaked meant a quick change of clothes to warm up before the rattan picnic basket was opened and the boiled egg sandwiches, apples, jam sandwiches and hot cocoa were eaten and drunk, sitting on sun warmed rocks.

Summer holidays meant mango and litchi season. At night when all was quiet except for the occasional nocturnal creature foraging in the garden or the ever-present crickets buzzing, we would hear the gardener bang on the brass thalis hanging from the trees, to ward off the fruit bats. They were the bane of all orchards, destroying the ripe mangoes as they swooped down in swarms on the fruit laden trees, sometimes destroying a full season's fruits in a single night.

Sidecars, Cows and Eucalyptus Trees

Doon was not just a holiday place but one with a colourful family history. Many stories originated from there, some of which preceded us. The funniest one was about my grandpa and his beloved Enfield with its wobbly sidecar. He loved riding this bike and decided to take granny on a joy ride one afternoon in their younger days, uphill down dale on the hilly roads of Doon. Off they went on their adventurous ride, their children waving them off from the house . An hour later the Enfield's roar was heard approaching home. When the kids saw Grandpa, they exclaimed in fright "where's Ma?". Grandpa frowned in puzzlement and said "She's right here" only to turn around and see the sidecar was missing! He muttered to himself "Oh that's why she stopped answering me" and off he went to retrace his steps. When he saw my granny in the detached sidecar, drunkenly resting on two wheels, a mile away from home, he apparently asked her indignantly, "Why on earth are you sitting here in the middle of the road?" She was speechless with anger! Needless to say, she never rode that sidecar again!

My mom's grandmother, who they named 'Tannamonu' for some odd reason, had lived in the Doon house long before we came along. She was a devout lady, who would pour over the prayer books and hymnals stacked in her room. Legend has it that she had a quick temper so the kids avoided her but enjoyed annoying her as well. Mom had a pet goat who ate anything vaguely edible so they let him loose in the old lady's room when she had stepped out. He made mincemeat of her prayer books, leaving tell-tale droppings on the floor and fled to the safety of the outdoors when he heard her voice. The house resounded with her yells and screams much to the children's joy. They were duly punished but were quite unrepentant, rewarding the goat with extra treats for his naughtiness.

The trees at Doon, especially the guava ones were easy to climb and I enjoyed shimmying up to hide and also view the world below from my high vantage point. Unfortunately, one time I climbed up onto the roof of the garage and found myself unable to get back down. My shouts brought the whole family out and amid much laughter from my brother and threats from my mom, I was brought down by the gardener, and put under house arrest for the rest of the day!

Another time when I was around five or six years old, grandpa took us out for our ritual morning walk. I was bundled up in a red woolly coat, with a red cap pulled down around my ears and thick itchy red woolen leggings to keep me warm. A few meters down the road we spotted a herd of cows grazing in a field. My bright red outfit caught the eye of a curious cow and he began trotting up towards me perhaps mistaking me for a juicy fruit! Stories of matadors and bulls chasing red flags flashed before my eyes and I fled screaming down the road with my brother in hot pursuit and the bemused cow chasing us, with grandpa alternately laughing and trying to fend off the four-legged creature. We landed inside our garden in a heap of tears and laughter. It took me a while to live that one down!

The boundaries of our garden on either side, were marked with aromatic and smooth eucalyptus trees. The fallen leaves created a fragrant carpet underfoot which we'd enjoy picnicking on. Grandma had bottled the oil from the trees and every sniffle was treated with the fragrant essence. I would imagine koalas eating it's leaves as a treat in their native land, Tasmania, where the eucalyptus originates. Another place that had many beautiful trees and shrubs was the FRI or the Forest Research Institute. We would drive down there occasionally to pick up plants from the nursery or simply to walk around the incredible grounds.

Dehradun was still a sleepy hill town those days, with limited attractions in the marketplace. One of them was the local bakery and its incredibly-crumbly melt-in-your-mouth *nankhatai* biscuits (shortbread biscuits) and freshly baked bread. The other was a milk shake and ice cream shop. The most coveted store was the book shop. We picked up quite a few books there to keep ourselves entertained through our month-long vacation. We also equipped ourselves with maps to plot our treks in the surrounding hills. Armed with a compass and binoculars we'd imagine ourselves to be adventurous travelers in an undiscovered land (though never far away from our grandparents or parents should we actually get lost!).

One winter when I was around six, my grandpa decided that we must learn Rabindra sangeet, waking us up at daybreak, bundling us into our winter jackets, before marching us down to a raised platform in the orchard at the back. Out would come the harmonium and copies of the Gitobitan, but despite his earnest efforts, thanks to the myriad adventures awaiting us, he could never get us to sit still long enough to sing. A few days into our lessons, he gave up and left us to our devices. He was legendarily strict and scary if the tales about him were true, but he was no match for our beguiling pleas to be let off to play.

Badminton, Fossils and an Orangutan

Our immediate neighbors in Ranchi were a lovely warm family of three, the Chowdhurys, with a wonderfully interesting house filled with antiques and fascinating archaeological finds. The older gentleman of the two brothers who lived there had been the Indian Ambassador to many fabulous far-off places and he regaled us with amazing stories of his travels.

From driving across Africa with an orphaned orangutan baby on his lap, to participating in archaeological digs in Egypt, he kept us enthralled with his tales. Mr Chowdhury senior loved animals and was a keen conservationist. He described in vivid detail, his interaction with the baby orangutan, who he cradled and bottle fed on the drive to the rescue-center. He even jokingly asked if he had begun resembling the orangutan because he had heard that people begin looking like their favourite animals. He was also a keen archaeologist and had an amazing fossil collection. Dada's love of history and archaeology grew in the company of this gentleman, who presented my brother with the tools of his first dig in Egypt.

We would go across for tea and games of scrabble and chess while listening to snippets of senior Mr Chowdhury's wonderfully adventurous life. He was a font of information about the world at large, and being a history buff, shared many interesting stories of the past. And the teas we were treated to by the younger brother's wife were scrumptious and plentiful. The delicate sandwiches, scones, cookies and cakes served on fine China with silver forks and embroidered napkins made us feel rather grown up and special.

Morabadi Hill, just a short walk away, was a regular haunt. We would often go up the winding stony path to the temple-like structure on top, accompanied by books and our camera to shoot photographs of the surrounding hills and the wild flowers. The most fascinating plant we found was the *lajjabati lata* popularly known as the 'touch me not' plant. Its delicate green leaves would fold shut the minute they were touched, as though in shyness or self-defense. There were also bushes of pretty yellow, pink and orange *putus* (lantana) flowers growing wild everywhere and lots of different ferns and trees. Mango trees grew in profusion in Ranchi, as well as the ever-present guavas.

We were pretty keen on playing badminton as kids. In Ranchi we found a few kids to play with, close to the house, in Morabadi. Our grandparent's house was at the base of the Morabadi (Tagore) Hill and half way up a house belonging to the Tagore family had been temporarily converted into a hostel for St Xavier's students who were also keen badminton players. So most afternoons a few spirited games took place and because I was significantly younger than the others, I got away with murder.

One late afternoon, we decided on climbing up the hill for an unscheduled game with the boys and set off in high spirits. Half way up hill to the hostel, a very drunk scruffy man leapt onto the rough path we were climbing and grabbed my arm demanding that we give him whatever money we had. We were kids! We had no money whatsoever and Dada grabbed my other arm and tried freeing me. Another disreputable looking chap appeared and grabbed hold of Dada. The scuffling and our yells and cries reached the ears of the boys in the hostel and they came racing down, to help us escape the clutches of these ruffians.

Dada urged me in Bangla to free myself and run down towards home. I did just that while the boys distracted and fought the two men but unfortunately, I tripped on a rock and tore a ligament on my ankle when I somehow freed my arm from the grasp of my captor. Despite the pain I hobbled home as fast as I could and related our tale of woe to my horrified grandparents. By the time I reached back my ankle had grown to the size of a medium football and was an interesting and very angry shade of purplish red. A search party went forth to rescue Dada but the brave hostel boys had freed him and sent the hoodlums packing. They brought Dada home as soon as they could, worried that I may have not made it back in one piece. The twisted ankle put paid to further badminton matches on that trip. It was back to sedentary board games and ice packs under the solicitous care of my grandparents.

To the left of the estate, we had a rather odd neighbor who though appearing to be a timid and self-effacing man, had a very scary 'pet' that even his family kept at a safe distance. We never understood why they had tried to domesticate it, because it was rather fierce and terrifying to look at. It was a full-grown, wild-eyed hyena that had been rescued as a pup. It looked extremely unpredictable even though we were assured he wouldn't charge at us, but the spines running down his back stood up whenever he saw strangers approach and his snarl and hair raising laugh-like howl was enough to keep us from repeated visits.

Leather Suitcases, Books and Hair Pins

Going to New Market with my maternal grandparents was an experience like no other. My maternal grandpa was a very large tall man (at least to my 2 feet of existence at the time) and holding his hand and running along beside him was fun. His booming voice would scatter all the stray vendors at the main entrance trying to sell us hangers and clothes pins. My grandma would be a step behind, shielded by his presence as she window shopped and occasionally stopped to buy odds and ends.

Didama (my maternal grandma) had long hair she did up in a complex bun, but to help her keep it in place, there were a host of secret pins and combs embedded out of sight within its coils. There were two shops in the main alley that sold pre-made buns, wigs, fake hair extensions and all the bells and bobs needed by ladies. We would make a stop at these shops which were more like little stalls clinging to the edges of the stores behind them. Here grandma bought her Bobby pins and fine wiry combs and long wavy u-shaped pins.

Next stop suitcase shop. For some reason Dehradun Dadu was always in need of a new suitcase whenever he visited Calcutta. Not just any suitcase. A pure leather one with brass buckles and leather straps and those triangular corner patches with brass buttons to make them stronger. No 'plastic' VIP boxes for him. But buying a leather suitcase was fraught with all kinds of unexpected consequences.

Dadu would first feel the leather for its genuineness, open the suitcase to inspect the pockets and compartments inside, hold it up to check its weight, and only then begin showing an interest in buying. One time an eager and foolish shopkeeper, anxious to sell him a suitcase declared that the chosen one was "strong enough to stand on" without quite realising that Dadu would take him at his word and jump on it with all his 6-foot 2 inch height and 120 kilo weight! Naturally, it collapsed.

My grandma loved reading and we'd make a stop at the bookshops for her to potter around and order the volumes she wanted. She enjoyed reading the stories of Sarat Chandra Chattopadhyay and Bankim Chandra Chattopadhyay and would make me read them to her, to better my knowledge of Bangla. My paternal grandma on the other hand, read *Thakurmar Jhuli* and *Aboltabol* to me much to my delight. My favourite was the much thumbed, frayed copy of *Hajabarala* I had inherited from Baba. I never tired of the nonsense inside its pages!

But I digress. We would move on to the crockery stores towards the side and back where we were greeted like long lost royalty and given wooden stools to sit on, which had to be moved around to stop tottering on the uneven floor of New Market. Once comfortably seated, the tea sets and dinner plates would be displayed for grandma's approval. Flowered designs with fine gold lines around the rims, fine China from Bengal Pottery, frilled ceramic cups, dinner plates with simple and elaborate designs and finally 'imported' China would be displayed. Once chosen, the cups and plates would be packed with straw and paper in sturdy boxes to be taken home.

Fish, Flowers and Waxpol Polish

The days I woke up by 6, I would hear my Dida singing a *Brohmo-sangeet* (Bengali devotional music in praise of Brahmā), to greet the morning. My room and attached balcony were mirror images of hers and both on the first floor so we would often communicate across the courtyard from our rooms. Her singing meant I needed to give her time to ready herself for breakfast before I could nip across so I busied myself with getting ready to meet her later.

I had two choices: I could run down the highly polished flight of stairs and risk slipping down the last few or I could climb onto the shiny teak banister and slide all the way down (and risking falling off the end when I reached the bottom)! My mother had the floors and all the woodwork regularly polished with good old Mansion Floor & Wood Polish that came in a round red tin. Though the floors gleamed and doors shone, it was easier to run a few steps and slide the rest of the way than to walk gracefully across the floors.

Talking of shiny surfaces reminds me of our monthly car washing day. Once a month my Baba would wash and polish our cars, till they gleamed with pride and on those mornings, we had our fill of playing with water and liquid soap. Our infamous bun-shaped Austin Somerset and the Ambassador would be parked in the driveway and the garden hose hooked up to wash the cars down. A bucket of suds and sponges, two children, a playful dog and an adult made quite a mess of themselves and the surroundings but the cars shone like new after they dried and were polished with Waxpol Auto polish in the bright orange tin. I can clearly recall the smell of the smooth waxy polish and soft yellow buffing cloths we shone the cars with. The white corduroy seat covers would be changed for fresh ones and the insides of the cars cleaned as well.

If it was an alternate Sunday, off we would go to Baba's factory, to fish. He had two large ponds on the premises, filled with all kinds of fish. Katla, Rui, Bata and tons of tiny Mourola. Twice a month, local fishermen came with their nets to catch a few for us. We would sit on the grassy bank of the larger pond with our fishing rods and try and catch fish with either bits of dough or squirmy earthworms (which I for one, refused to touch!).

The early morning cool air, birds chirping in the tall grass, the occasional splashes and ripples caused by jumping fish and the muted sounds of people in the houses behind the factory lulled me into a dreamlike state and the sudden tug at the end of my fishing rod would take me by surprise. My Baba taught us how to bait hooks and swing the rod over our heads to reach the deeper parts of the pond. I can't recall if I ever caught any fish large enough to eat but the joy of spending a quiet morning by the pond was an adventure in itself.

Another occasional Sunday ritual was visiting the wholesale flower market below the Calcutta end of the Howrah Bridge.

Ma would drive us to the Mullick Ghat flower market early in the morning, to get the freshest flowers that had arrived overnight from far off places. The ghat used to be known as Nimai Mullick Ghat, built by Rammohan Mullick in 1855, in memory of his father Nimai Charan Mullick. It was built on the grounds of the old 'Noyaner Ghat', built by Noyanchand Mullick, in 1793. Another famous Mullick family member, Jadunath Mullick, renovated the ghat between 1870-74.

A pontoon bridge was built across the river to the south of the present ghat around this time, linking Howrah to Calcutta. The Howrah Bridge did not exist at that time. The Jagannath Ghat, built by Shobharam Basak in 1760, stands right next to the Mullick Ghat. Ferries would take pilgrims to the Jagannath Temple in Puri, from these two ghats, and perhaps that is why the flower market developed here, to provide fresh flowers to the pilgrims as offerings to the gods they were about to visit and worship.

We would make our way to the rose sellers, and those that sold carnations, gerberas and gladioli. These were the flowers we liked the most. We learnt to distinguish between the various kinds of roses, like the naturally grown and more perishable blousy red and deep red blossoms from their more elegant cousins, the hybrid pink and yellow ones that lasted longer. Carnations came in a variety of colours – pink, our favourite, red, white and yellow as well as a white variety that was rimmed with red. The gerberas always looked so cheerful, in their individual cellophane collars that held the petals closed, as if they were bursting with energy to fling their gaily colored petals open to greet the day. The sea of pink, orange, yellow, white and shades of red made it tough for us to restrict our buying to just one bunch. Gerberas never lasted for more than a day or two as though they tired easily after their energetic beginning that drained all their energy. After all it must have been hard for them to stay cheerful and keep smiling forever!

I once met our school 'flower man' there, with his round flat wicker basket filled with the blooms we liked buying for our teachers on special occasions. Baby's breath, carnations and roses vied for space with small bunches of ferns that he used to make pretty posies for us. He would sit just outside the junior school gate, arranging the flowers in neat rows on a sheet of paper laid out on a plastic sheet on the sidewalk, alongside the 'sticker man' who sold a variety of highly desirable sticky pictures of flowers, animals and cartoon characters. We were not allowed to attach these to our brown paper covered school exercise books but they would festoon our tiffin boxes, water bottles, and pencil cases. We would try reaching school early to use the few extra minutes to browse this collection and implore our parents to buy us some.

Grundig, Wynton Marsalis and a Shaky Old Building

The Grundig turntable was the star of all parties at home. My father made sure that we always had a spare head in case the needle got spoilt with use. Every few months we would wash our records with a mild detergent and water solution and dry them out carefully ensuring that no lint remained on the surface.

Under the turntable stored in groups by genre were the LPs, 78 and 45 RPM records of my parents' collection. Anyone travelling from UK had to pay a visit to Tower Records in Piccadilly and pick up a few vinyls for us. Lots of Big Band jazz, and of course the greats like Coltrane and Miles Davis and later Wynton Marsalis made themselves heard.

Von Karajan the brilliant Austrian conducting the Berlin Philharmonic was a top choice. We had collected all 9 symphonies by Beethoven and would listen to them often. I really loved the Baroque composers and listened with rapt attention to Bach and Vivaldi, attempting to play Bach's concertos on the piano.

Talking of the piano reminds me of the instrument we had at home and its history. My Doon Dadu had bought it for his children but apart from my uncle no one played it. So, when I came around my Ma had it transported from Doon to Howrah. An upright piano, it shone with the patina of age, and its innards fascinated me. I would often open the front and watch the tiny hammers strike the strings on the back board as I played the corresponding keys. It all seemed rather magical.

My piano classes began at school when I was 6, and a lovely gentle blue eyed Irish nun was my first teacher. I had to be lifted onto the piano stool, my legs being too short to climb the bench and the pedals were way beyond my reach. The music rooms above and behind the stage of our main hall at school were quite quaint. Each one had a piano and with the wooden floor and low ceiling, felt like a cozy wooden box, the only trace of the surroundings being the faint voices of girls playing basketball in the courts below.

After my teacher left for Ireland, I began my lessons at the Calcutta School of Music on Wellesley Street. Now that building was the shakiest structure I've ever been inside. It trembled with every passing car but the wonderful original wooden floors and elaborate molded plaster ceilings gave it the grace of an old but aristocratic lady. It had tall green wooden shutters and large rooms with high ceilings and the building echoed with the strains of the pianos, violins and cellos being played inside. Every step of the sweeping wooden staircase creaked, the marble floors in the foyer and upstairs were uneven and cracked with age but the building had an otherworldly charm that no new house would ever have.

My last teacher was a wonderful, colourful and rather beautiful lady whose apartment in Palace Court I went to for my lessons. The combination of fresh flowers, books and artefacts made her home both warm and inviting. I loved her music appreciation classes and continued with my lessons till she retired to Darjeeling.

Chameleons, Squirrels and Fantailed Pigeons

We had many visitors to our garden at home. Some made quite an impression on me, with their shenanigans. A pair of scary looking chameleons appeared one day, looking for a place to sun themselves while remaining hidden from sight. I saw them sitting on a red brick at the edge of the lawn and they had changed colour to a reddish pink to remain camouflaged or perhaps to absorb the light. Another time they were a bright green colour, sitting on the verdant grass, their long tongues flicking out in quick movements to catch unsuspecting insects. I must admit I never went too close to them despite Gerald Durrell assuring me that they were harmless. They looked like fire breathing miniature dragons, ready to attack anytime they were approached.

Another time, someone's pet badger found its way into our garden. We discovered it in the funniest way. I was playing with my stuffed toys, sitting on the cool floor of my bedroom on a warm summer day. I had ranged them around me in a circle and was pretending to teach them simple math. My ayah walked in on us with my lunch and sat down next to me to convince me to eat. I insisted that she feed my furry friends as well and when she turned her attention to them, one animal blinked! She let out a blood curdling yell, grabbed me and the plate of food and ran out of the room yelling *"bhodor bhodor"* much to everyone's astonishment! Apparently, the badger had sneaked into my room and sat down next to the teddy, hoping perhaps to learn a table or two! When my ayah went back my room, she noticed he had a red collar and realised he was someone's pet. He was shooed into the garden and eventually returned to his owner who came looking for his wandering badger.

The house behind ours had a flock of pale-coloured birds, probably pigeons, that flew around freely, circling our house occasionally, especially when the *mali* (gardener) scattered seeds for them in the courtyard, tempting them to come for a tasty snack. One day I noticed that amongst them were two white fantailed pigeons, strutting around looking important. They had every reason to feel proud with their lovely tail feathers fanning out in a circle behind them. Unlike their ordinary cousins they walked on their toes adding to the aura of appearing superior!

We had a large cage with blue and green budgerigars who were very pretty but quite noisy. I felt sorry for them because they were living behind bars but Ma said if I released them, they would be killed by the crows and kites.

One time while reading a book in my room, I heard a knocking on the window and opening it found a curious baby squirrel peering up at me. It seemed quite unafraid so I quickly got some peanuts to feed it and it kept coming back for more till its mom probably told him to stay away from humans. It had the bushiest tail and bright eyes and sat up on its haunches to eat the peanuts, holding them with both its tiny hands. At times it would stuff a few nuts for later, into its tiny cheeks.

Gerald Durrell had a deep impact on my imagination and I dreamt of travelling to Corfu to join him on his adventures. In the meantime, I made up travel adventures of my own with the birds and animals in our garden.

Ice packs, Bread Pudding and Sati

My maternal aunt and her husband lived in Jodhpur while he was Chief Engineer, Rajasthan Ground Water Board. Our holidays in Rajasthan were epic, thanks to the frequent tours he went on across the state. My brother and I accompanied my aunt and uncle on one tour that took us to Udaipur via Bhilwara, Nathdwara and then Mount Abu and back to Jodhpur by car.

It was hot! The car, an Ambassador, was fitted with curtains and fans but those didn't help. So, every morning when we set off, we would buy several kilos of ice and pack them in plastic bags to use as ice packs! It was the craziest car trip I've ever been on! There we were, two adults and two kids and a driver, bowling along the dusty highways, speeding past camels and gaily dressed Rajasthani women singing songs, with fast melting ice packs on our heads, towels on our necks to avoid getting drenched, laughing our heads off at the strange stares of villagers in creaky, sandy, colourful but dusty busses carrying people, chickens and the odd goat or two!

Several stops were made every day to replenish our stock of cold beverages. We would also gulp down glasses of *ganney ki ras* or fresh sugarcane juice, *lassi* (drink made with curd) and cold water at *dhabas*, (roadside eateries) ending our days at the most incredible Circuit Houses.

The one in Udaipur was up above the lake. A beautiful white building with high ceilings and enormous rooms, very dimly lit, and long echoing corridors. It was reputed to be haunted but unfortunately, we didn't meet any ghosts! Perhaps it was too hot even for the resident spirits who were probably hovering over the lake to cool themselves. Despite the thick walls and high ceilings, it was so hot inside that the bedsheets burned against our skin. We came up with a plan: we sprinkled many bottles of cold water on the beds, and watched the steam rising, drying up in minutes under the fans. We had to repeat the process till the beds cooled down enough to sleep on, repeating the process after a couple of hours!

Dinners at the circuit houses were fairly standard across Rajasthan. A choice of soups - mulligatawny/tomato/clear chicken broth with toasted bread wrapped in linen napkins, pats of butter on ice in little ceramic saucer-like bowls, roast chicken or fried fish with tartare sauce, mashed potato and boiled vegetables, ending with either custard and fruits or bread pudding. We were served by liveried waiters, much like in the Clubs of Calcutta.

We visited the Mehrangarh Fort at Jodhpur every time we went to my aunt's. What I remember other than the imposing structure of the fort high up on a hill, with strategically placed cannons and the walkway where the lookouts would keep watch, were 15 sets of handprints of the wives and concubines of Maharaja Man Singh who had been forced to commit sati when the Maharaja died.

The infamous 'sati marks' left quite an impression on me, as sati was one of the barbaric traditions that Raja Ram Mohan

Roy, the founder of the Brahmo Samaj we were members of, had helped abolish during the tenure of Lord Bentinck, the Governor General of India. I imagined the terror the poor women must have felt when they were forced to immolate themselves in the funeral pyre. Since women were seen as personal possessions, who had no place in society as widows, and were vulnerable to being attacked without a husband to protect them, death was seen as a merciful ending.

I suppose growing up Brahmo, hearing tales of the changes made in society by leaders of the Samaj, that benefitted girls and women, I felt rather lucky as a kid. I used to listen with rapt attention to stories about what led our various forefathers to join the Samaj. Both my parents were members of the Samaj, as were their parents and grandparents.

Legend has it that my mother's great grandfather who was born into a Kuleen Brahmin family (supposedly thought of as a high 'caste') had been married off to a hundred and ten women by his parents and village elders! Apparently, there was a dearth of male Kuleen Brahmins, and since marrying one assured a girl of an elevated status in her social circle, these hapless (or maybe not!) men were married off to heaps of young girls. Most of the time, the man had no inkling of these marriages, because the ceremonies could be carried out with just a simple inanimate object belonging to the man. And the girl could continue living as a 'married woman' in her parent's house, free from pity and ridicule, with an umbrella or wooden *kharams* (clogs) belonging to and representing her spouse.

Now some men would take advantage of this absurd and unfair tradition, by travelling from one 'wife's' house to another, claiming their marital rights and being feted by their in-laws, who considered themselves blessed by their very presence. Feasts would be organised and long forgotten relatives would be invited to meet the man and his incredibly 'lucky' wife. Ma's great grand-father who was a learned and fairly 'modern man' and had married his childhood sweetheart of his own volition, took umbrage when he learnt of his multiple wives married to him on the quiet. He left his family home with the only wife he acknowledged as legitimately his, and travelled to the nearest town, joining the Brahmo Samaj when he realised that he was more in tune with their teaching and beliefs than those held dear by his regressive family.

Another ancestor, my paternal grandma's grandmother joined the Samaj after a particularly traumatic incident that had a deep impact on her hitherto unshaken beliefs. She was a staunch devotee of Goddess Kali, the Goddess of darkness, destruction, and death. Kali is also a symbol of Mother Nature, believed to represent the creation of life and the universe as well. One fateful morning, when this lady entered her 'puja' room with its life size idol of her Goddess, she was greeted by an awful sight. Kali's eyes had been gouged out by some animal through the night and she bore deep scratches on her arms and face from her encounter. Having prayed to the Goddess for years to keep her family safe, she was devastated that her beloved Kali had been unable to protect herself and consequently couldn't be relied upon to look after anyone else! Her faith shaken by this incident; she eventually joined the Brahmo Samaj as her belief in the power of idol worship faded over time.

There were many interesting incidents like these that changed the course of the two family's lives and beliefs, eventually leading all its members to the Brahmo Samaj.

Sticky Blue Plumbago and a Furry White Tail

Sticky blue plumbago flowers on a white plume waving in my face brought me awake…I could sense alert black eyes following my movements as I stretched and smiled, waiting for the wet nosed 'boop' and there it was! The final call to wake up and greet the sunny afternoon as I lazed below the bright bottlebrush blooms. As I squinted up at the sky, I ran my fingers over the soft grass. Time to water the lawn and check if the black and red striped caterpillars had begun to turn into butterflies.

When I was around twelve, my Pishima (father's sister) called one day to say she had a surprise for me, and I needed to collect it personally from her in-law's house in Dasnagar. My Mom drove my best friend Chumki and I, both buzzing with excitement, to their place and we were directed to the terrace garden. I thought I'd never been happier when I saw what Pishima had in store for me. There were several white fluffy balls of fur tumbling over one another in a pen amongst the flowers, with an indulgent mama looking on. As we went up to them one puppy waddled his way towards me as I stepped into the pen, and sat down on my foot. When I picked up the pup, Pishima laughed and said that the puppy had obviously taken to me and this was the one she had chosen for me anyway. Ma had apparently mentioned that we'd prefer a male, and he was the only male in the litter.

That night and for quite a few sleepless nights afterwards, Chumki and I fussed over him, naming him 'Bhombol Das', feeding him, comforting him when he whimpered and marveling at his adorable face. Bhombol grew to be a handsome dog, really playful and a perfect companion, accompanying me everywhere on all my imaginary adventures.

My furry playmate chased a yellow bird as it flew up into the magenta and burnt orange bougainvillea climbing up towards the sun. Faint traces of my Dida's voice reached out to me as I dozed off again, with my arms around Bhombol. "Time to water the lawn. The sun is setting and it's cooler now. Remember to water the sunflowers in the back. They look thirsty. And fill up the birdbath. The sparrows and crows need to keep cool too." Was she talking to me? Yes! I'd better get up and do as she's asked.

Dida was sitting on a leather 'mora' (stool) at the far end of the garden, an umbrella protecting her delicate and easily burnt skin from the afternoon sun. She handed me the 'khurpi' (gardening trowel) to dig up the tiny weeds on the lawn, and flower beds. As I unrolled the green hose and attached it to the brass tap still warm to the touch from the summer sun, my attention was caught by the chatty call of the tiny hummingbirds that often visited our garden. They chirped a mile a minute, flitting from flower to flower.

Watering the lawn took a while because Bhombol kept tugging at the hose as it snaked over the grass, convinced it was a live animal waiting to play with him. The sticky blue plumbago flowers adorning his tail had been added to with bits of mud and leaves from the damp lawn. Rather than hosing him down I'd have to bathe him indoors or he would surely roll around on the lawn and ruin my efforts to keep him clean!

Bridges, Cows and Caramel Custard

My maternal Grandfather, who had been in the North Western Railways shared a lot of stories of his travels and adventures by train. Since he was a fairly senior official, he had a special coach, with a living room, bedrooms, a dining room and pantry which would be hitched onto which ever train he needed to travel by. The family would travel in style, with personal attendants and other comforts of home. Once, when my mother and her siblings had been quite young, their train met with an accident at night. Their coach did not suffer any damages, but my uncle who was a baby at the time, got lost in the confusion. There was no sign of him anywhere, much to everyone's consternation. After several hours spent frantically searching for him, my grandma found him fast asleep, bundled up in his blanket, under a seat behind a water cooler.

The transition from coal fed engines to electrical trains made a huge difference! No more soot, a smoother ride and faster trains. I remember the smell of the soot that the engines would belch out. It was exciting to see the engine when the track curved enough for the front to be visible from our compartment. The horn announcing our presence to whoever was listening, the plume of black smoke, the occasional level crossing with a line of impatient cyclists, hay-laden lorries, a car or two and a few villagers on produce-laden carts yoked to a couple of bullocks with kids waving at the passing train, all made for a feeling of importance, as though the world around us was waiting for us to pass as we sped on to our destination.

Bridges over rivers flowing below changed the tone of the train as it sped through metallic crisscross struts. The rhythm altered and I always held my breath till we safely reached the far shore, never quite sure that the iron frame would be strong enough to carry the weight of the enormous train. But the sight of rivers were a welcome relief from the acres and acres of fields. The green of Bengal with its water filled rice plantations transitioned to drier landscapes, the further north we traveled. Wheat and corn took over and the animals too looked different. The smaller cows of Bengal were replaced by the tougher and taller 'Multani' cows. The coconut trees and ponds were no longer visible as evergreens and fruit trees took their place.

The presence of tunnels on our journey were thrilling. Suddenly the train would be plunged into darkness, only lit by the dim blue tinted night lights that stayed on. The sound of the wheels echoed off the sides of the tunnel carved out of the hill, lending an air of mystery as though there was a second ghost train on our heels.

At night the darkness of rural India enveloped us as we prepared for dinner and sleep. On the Doon Express, the second night meant food from the railway canteen car. The tomato soup, roast chicken, boiled vegetables, two pieces of bread and butter and finally either ice cream or caramel custard would round off our day.

Singer Sewing Machines, Buttons and a Purse

I woke up to a steady squeak, squeak, squeak followed by a rapid clackity clack, clack, clack and I knew it was the sound of Ma pedaling the sewing machine and wondered if she was making me a new dress or a pinafore. I loved pinafores specially the ones with pockets. I could carry around so many things in them. Rocks from the river bed in Doon, shells I had picked up in Puri or sweets I wanted the freedom to savor while playing in the garden or *uthon*.

Ma had a pretty black and gold machine with a foot pedal and a shiny metal wheel with a thick cord that connected it to a bigger wheel below. I remember that the cord was joined by a thick metal pin like a staple which would at times get caught in the wheels and need to be hammered back in place. I enjoyed watching her sewing stuff on it and later I began making dresses for my dolls, making sure I didn't get my fingers caught under the rapidly moving needle. I learnt how to thread it and make sure the bobbin had enough thread to see me through what I was stitching.

The drawer underneath had a wealth of coloured threads, buttons and hooks and a big pair of tailoring scissors which Ma used to cut cloth in the patterns she got from her sewing books and the Woman's Wear magazines. Sometimes when she discarded these magazines, I would carefully cut out the dresses and pin them on to paper cutout dolls I created. I had a boxful of these dolls and enjoyed mixing and matching their outfits, to match mine.

Ma had a square metallic tea caddy with lots of buttons inside. The caddy had a painting of a bouquet of flowers on its cover which had over time become slightly crooked and didn't close properly, scattering buttons all over the place if I wasn't careful. I loved playing with the colourful buttons inside and with the ribbons and pieces of lace that were kept aside to add to my dresses.

There was one particular shop in New Market, towards the back that specialised in these things and we would carry my dress materials to buy matching laces and ribbons for them. The shop was filled with rows upon rows of stuff to add to dresses, from bows and flowers made from satin ribbons, to colored lace and buttons of all sizes and colours.

I remember Dada stitching a purse on the sewing machine. It was made from a piece of denim cut from Baba's old jeans, which made it rather difficult to sew, being so thick. But he managed it and we gave it to Ma on her birthday. We were all of 10(me) and 13 (Dada). The purse looked a little crooked and the stitching a bit rough but Ma loved it nevertheless!

Victoria Amazonica, Mad Trees and Sher Shah Suri

The Botanical Gardens in Shibpur being so close to home, were a regular haunt, and we often took out of town visitors and friends from across the Hooghly River, to show them the rare plants that it was famous for such as the Great Banyan Tree. With its large number of aerial roots, growing from its horizontal branches to stretch vertically to the ground, the grand evergreen looked more like a dense forest than a single tree. It is more than 250 years old now, and has weathered many cyclones from as far back as 1864. The original tree trunk had to be removed in 1925 when it got infected with a life-threatening disease but the tree survived and thrives even today.

This garden, stretching for miles along the riverside, was established in 1786 by Colonel Robert Kyd, a British officer who was a keen botanist, to identify new plants that could turn profitable for the British, such as teak and spices, not to simply collect rare plants as objects of mere curiosity. The East India Company's Court of Directors supported Kyd's ambitions to grow cinnamon, tobacco, dates, Chinese tea, and coffee in the garden as well as cacti such as Nopal which was imported from Mexico to produce textile dyes, an industry which Spain dominated at that time. The garden was a place of both horticultural experiment and commercial venture.

After some research I learnt that a certain Joseph Dalton Hooker, a famous botanist and a close friend of Sir Charles Darwin wrote of the Botanical gardens: "Amongst its greatest triumphs may be considered the introduction of the tea-plant from China … the establishment of the tea-trade in the Himalayas and Assam is almost entirely the work of the superintendents of the gardens of Calcutta and Saharanpur," where a second 'Company Garden' was established to experiment on and promote commercially viable plants. History aside, the garden was a beautiful place. I loved walking down the soaring avenue of tall royal palm trees that stretched all the way to the riverside. They looked so stately, standing proud in orderly rows like an honour-guard welcoming important visitors.

As one reached the river, a long stretch of road opened up with small water bodies and parkland on the right, planted with varieties of plants and trees growing in orderly groups. All kinds of palms, some bearing edible fruits, others capable of storing drinkable water in their bulbous trunks and a host of exotic trees dotted the garden… there was the strange looking Mad Tree, which had leaves in different shapes and sizes, perhaps thus named because it looked a little crazy. Then there was the Sausage Tree with its salami like fruit hanging in clusters as if in a butcher's shop and the Cannon Ball Tree more commonly known as *Nagalinga* with its ball shaped fruits and round red flowers that grew directly from its trunk.

I was amazed to find the national tree of Madagascar, the Baobab Tree, also known as the 'tree of heaven' and 'tree of life' in the garden. The Baobab provides not just vast amounts of water stored in its trunk, useful in drought ridden places, its leaves are a source of vitamin C and its fruits are not just edible, but are also rich in vitamins, proteins, antioxidants and minerals. Legend has it that Arabian traders, in awe of its life-giving qualities, took saplings back home, and also introduced it to the Egyptians, before it travelled to Asia and other parts of the world.

Beautiful flowering aquatic plants grew in the ponds, such as the Victoria Amazonica Water Lily with its huge round leaves, probably the largest in the world, glistening with drops of water as they provided the perfect foil for the pretty pink flowers growing in their midst. Its leaves were big enough to support the weight of a small child. The green leaves had raised rims exposing the bright purple corrugated surface underneath, facing the water.

There were plenty of places to sit and watch the river but my favourite was atop the horizontal branch of a tree that dipped down to the water flowing sluggishly below. My brother and I were keen photographers, and spent hours shooting interesting close ups of flowers and gnarly tree trunks with bumpy bark enveloping them. Back home we had set up a dark room with all the paraphernalia for developing the black and white film rolls we used, pouring over the negatives to print the most interesting shots. I remember the awe with which we watched prints come to life in the developing tray. We shot mostly in black and white because the contrasts made the images look so much more interesting and intense.

Living on the Grand Trunk Road, which is where my grandfather and Dad had built our house, I always felt as though I was linked by association to a great historical feat. Legendarily built by Sher Shah Suri, the G T Road was originally a 2500km road, known variously as Sadak-e-Azam, Badshahi Sarak and Sadak-e-Sher Shah over the years. Eventually, the British renamed it the Grand Trunk Road as we know of it today.

According to the Encyclopedia Britannica, of which we were great admirers, pouring over the leather covered volumes with avid interest, this highway was built along an ancient route called Uttarapatha built by Chandragupta Maurya in the 3rd century BC stretching from the mouth of the Ganges to the north-western frontier of India. Further improvements to this road were made under Ashoka. The old route was re-aligned by Sher Shah Suri to stretch from Peshawar in Pakistan through India all the way to Sonargaon in Bangladesh. We often went on road trips to Ranchi, to my paternal grandparent's place, and once all the way to Dehradun, and if I remember correctly, we drove along GT Road which was in parts the same route followed by various National Highways.

GT road had enormous trees on either side, some planted at the time of Sher Shah to provide shade to travelers. The lovely green canopy created a cool tunnel to drive through, the play of light filtering in through the leaves creating a pretty pattern on the on the road. Originally Sher Shah had planted fruit trees to provide food for travelers and had had wells installed for drinking water along the way. Some of these trees, lost in storms and from disease had been replaced by flowering Gulmohors, and huge Banyan trees with multiple hanging aerial roots that sometimes swept the tops of buses and lorries passing below. Over time villagers had built temples and places to rest under the banyan trees.

I used to imagine the relief that 'runners' who sometimes doubled as 'town criers' must have felt as they rested under shade trees and quenched their thirst from wells and streams nearby before speeding off on their journeys to convey important news and letters to heads of states and other dignitaries in Sparta, Greece, England and eventually Colonial India. I was reminded of the haunting verses of the Bengali song *"Runner Chutechey Tai Jhum Jhum Ghonta Bajey Ratey"* sung by Hemanta Mukherjee in his amazing baritone, commemorating the lonely and strenuous lives of runners as they ran tirelessly from place to place, the tinkling of bells on their feet the only sound of their relentless journeys, as they conveyed good news and bad, before the spread of literacy and the railways made their services obsolete.

Double Cream, Kalimpong Cheese and Eggs

A trip to New Market meant a whole afternoon of trailing behind my Ma while she stopped at various places and bought all that she'd put on her list. Our favourite coolie would come rushing to the car the minute we parked and would hoist his *tokri* (basket) on his turbaned head in preparation for our marketing spree.

First stop Poddar's Store. We were greeted with cold Thumbs Up and seated on their metal folding chairs. Out came the list as I gazed around at all the goodies around us. Imported hams, whole strawberry jams, marmalade, olives glistening in tall jars with red pimento centers, tins of cocoa, drinking chocolate and slabs of cooking chocolate. My eyes would glaze over after a while and I'd get restless to move on to the next stop.

Eggs! Rows upon rows of eggs. Brown desi eggs, big white poultry eggs. Even a few duck's eggs. An empty egg crate would be lined up and every single egg would be held up against a light bulb to make sure it passed muster before it was placed in the tray. A second tray would be placed on top and tied with strings to cradle the eggs securely in the Paper Mache trays.

Fruits and vegetables came next. From high up above the pile of vegetables, arranged in tiers, the shopkeeper would point out the choicest greens, the freshest tomatoes and celery stalks, young crunchy cucumbers, ripe orange pumpkins, and a whole host of Ma's favourite vegetables. I enjoyed the experience of perching atop a tall wooden stool while the buying took place, as I kept a lookout for the occasional mice and big brown cockroaches that scurried around under the stalls.

The days we went grocery shopping, there'd be no stops at shops carrying non edibles, because some of the things we bought were perishable, like chicken and butter. But before leaving New Market we had to buy some lovely smoky rounds of Bandel Cheese and the sharper Kalimpong one. One had to taste a sliver of the Kalimpong cheese to make sure it was still moist and fresh and only then would the big yellow wax coated wheel be cut to our requirements.

If it was not too late, a stop at Nahoum Confectioners was imperative to buy coconut flavoured macaroons, crackers infused with herbs, square almond cookies and loaves of freshly baked bread. In winter we bought rectangular dense fruit cakes as gifts for friends, with a packet or two of cheese straws thrown in.

Next stop, the cream shop near the flower stalls. If the menu at home included ice cream or sweet dishes with whipped cream, Ma would pick up the special double cream that came in heavy bottomed glass milk bottles with foil caps. The cream shop vendor was a portly, jolly, shiny cheeked man who looked like he feasted on lots of double cream himself! From his cross-legged perch atop the shiny clean aluminum counter, his tummy straining the buttons of his spotless white shirt worn with a blue checked lungi, he once asked my slender Mom with avuncular concern, "You buy so much cream but you don't look like you eat any of it yourself"!

I remember walking past the tall barber's chairs, on wooden platforms where shopkeepers and rickshaw pullers got shaved and spruced up by mustachioed barbers wielding wicked looking 'cut throat' knives, as a few children recited tables and wrote on slates in the tiny 'school' set up on the pavement. The barber doubled up as the teacher, keeping a strict eye on the kids, making sure they were paying attention to his instructions.

Airguns, Tigers and Trapeze Artists

The *uthon* was good for many things. Badminton matches in the early evenings with the net strung on poles between the two houses. Dida's and ours. Sometimes our pet Pomeranian ran off with the shuttlecock but that was part of the game! When the sun began setting, making it hard to see clearly, we'd switch on the outdoor lights and continue playing. My parents sometimes joined us if they didn't have parties to go to or guests coming over. Sometimes our cook and a house maid would be cajoled into partnering us and many hilarious moments followed as we tried teaching them the rules of the game.

When Baba bought us scooters, we would race up and down and around the *uthon*, trying our best not to bang into the enclosing walls or windows or skid on the grates covering the encircling drains. I would at times try driving with one of our dogs on the footboard, but the additional weight and his wriggles would often land us both in a giggling heap. Dada and I progressed to roller skates although the *uthon's* cement tiled surface wasn't smooth enough to skate without getting stuck in the grooves. Though the going was far smoother indoors, the polished floors resulted in skids and many banged elbows and knees. But the thrill of skating didn't stop us.

We set up a cork backed target in front of the door to the *koyla ghar* (a most frightening room filled with innumerable monsters hiding in the stacks of pitch-black coal). My brother and I practiced shooting at its red black and white concentric circles with our trusty air gun, retrieving the tiny lead bullets from the sandbag placed behind the target. We got pretty proficient at this and won ourselves quite a few toys at the melas in the maidan.

Talking of melas reminds me of the Gemini Circus that came around every year to the Howrah Maidan. Accompanied by a parent and a couple of members of our household, we would excitedly line up for tickets, while watching with fascination the colourful clowns, horses and gymnasts in shiny costumes outside the big tent with its colourful flags flapping in the breeze, as they readied themselves for the evening show.

Tigers roared, elephants impatiently pawed the dusty ground underfoot, lions paced up and down in their cages and monkeys rode on shoulders waiting for the audience to take their places inside the big gaudy tent festooned with tiny lights. The familiar strains of Baby Elephant's Walk could be heard over the excited chatter of the audience as we took our seats, the clowns driving around the ring in their gaily painted cars that collapsed into piles of tyres and metal pieces every so often. Though the clowns were entertaining, we looked forward to the performing animals, acrobats and jugglers, as we snacked on popcorn and chips on our wooden seats.

The trapeze artists climbed poles and sailed overhead from side to side, holding on to rings on ropes that looked too fragile to support them. I watched with fascination as they flung themselves with no regard for their safety from ring to ring to the outstretched hands of other gymnasts who caught them mid swing. Despite the safety nets I would worry about them and breathe sighs of relief when they completed their acts. My ayah's older daughter who was quite athletic, joined the Gemini Circus when she was around fifteen and toured with them all over the country. She eventually married a young lion tamer who joined the circus a few years later.

The lion and tiger tamers made the animals jump through hoops and perch on high stools like obedient children. Jugglers continued to juggle colourful balls as the dogs performed tricks, standing on their hind legs. Elephants would sometimes swoop up water from buckets placed within their reach, and playfully spray the audience as they strode around swaying to the beat of the music playing in the tent, as acrobats performed handstands on their broad backs. I marveled at the unicycle riders as they jumped onto one another's shoulders, forming human pyramids up in the air while circling the sawdust and sand covered ring.

Outside, the smell of popcorn and roasted peanuts filled the air, mixed with the heady aroma of candy floss being spun in clouds of pink on ice cream sticks. Vendors selling balloons, puppets, paper fans and sugary sweets hawked their wares as we gawped wide eyed at the crowds around us. Dada and I, held hands as we were shepherded out from the magical Maidan with its myriad treats, most of which we could only long for, begging for a wooden doll here or a colourful tin toy car there, till our pleas wore down the parent accompanying us. These toys seemed so much more exciting than the more sophisticated talking dolls and mechanical toy cars we had at home. Triumphantly holding aloft our prized purchases we would run home to share our excitement with our grandparents who oohed and ahh-ed at our new possessions.

Later at night when the music was silenced and the crowds dispersed, I could clearly hear the tigers and lions roar. It was strange to hear wild animals calling out in a city where the usual night time sounds were the haunting long-drawn-out horn of an occasional long- distance train or the far-off ships as they sailed into the harbor across the river.

Backing Trams, Swinging Trees and an Orange Flame

Driving in Calcutta is perilous. We had quite a few misadventures, not just involving potholes that pockmarked most roads in the city, but other cars, trams, and even a tree! There we were, Ma at the wheel of our trusty white Ambassador, driving back from school on the Howrah Bridge, trams trundling along in the middle lane serving as a divider between the two sides, buses with ear piercing air horns racing one another, bright yellow taxis piled with people and luggage zooming towards the station and lorries laden with everything from onions to cows, to bales of hay spilling out from all sides lurching from one pothole to another. Maneuvering through this chaos required not just driving skills but the ability to anticipate which car or bus or lorry would suddenly change lanes leaving you sputtering with rage as you braked to avoid hitting another vehicle.

When we reached the Howrah end of the bridge, and took a turn towards the station and eventually home, an almighty bang pushed our car into the next lane. An overladen lorry with a trailer carrying huge logs had side swiped us as it turned, and the edge of a tree trunk protruding out from the trailer landed on the roof of our car. Complete chaos ensued as Ma struggled to open her door, though luckily neither of us were injured. Policemen came running, passers-by rushed to our aid and the lorry driver was hauled out from his perch. Thankfully, other than an alarming looking dent on the roof of our car and scratches and grazes along the left side, we were unharmed, and after a while we drove home, after extricating the car from the tree trunk. I rushed in to relate our adventure to my Dad, opening my story with "A tree came and hit us". He began laughing, saying that he had heard many tall tales in his life, but this one topped the list!

Another time, while we were waiting behind a stationary tram at a red light on Strand Road, it suddenly began reversing in our direction. Ma frantically honked and tried backing out of the way, but we were hemmed in by other cars, and the tram banged into our bonnet, and kept going, pushing us along. People on the road yelled at the tram driver who was at the front end of the tram, to stop. He had been attempting to change tracks to go towards College Street. Trams have driving compartments at both ends precisely for the purpose of reversing, but this fellow decided to try the maneuver from the wrong end. Once again Baba laughed at our description of the incident, saying "Trams can't reverse", but he wasn't there to witness this anomaly!

The most dramatic car related incident happened one afternoon as we made our way home down Red Road. That afternoon there was a Mohun Bagan /East Bengal football match at the Mohun Bagan Club and the mounted police on their magnificent horses were out in full force to manage the crowds. There were a number of police vans lining the road, disgorging additional policeman to manage traffic once the game was over and the excitable crowds began spilling over onto the roads. As we drove down a police van suddenly took an illegal U turn right in front of our car, and Ma's quick response prevented us from hitting the van. Unfortunately, the driver of the car behind us didn't brake in time and crashed into us, smashing his radiator in the process. Ma jumped out of our car and ran to the back to examine the damage only to be confronted by a weeping uniformed driver wailing at the state of his car. He kept saying "My boss will never believe that this was not my fault." His car radiator had caved in and plumes of hot steam were spiraling up to the sky.

Ma, full of indignation, began racing after the police van trying to stop the driver from running away. There she was, in a flaming orange sari, *anchal* streaming behind her like a flame, surrounded by cars and mounted policemen, racing down Red Road much to the astonishment of other drivers. Realising that she'd be faster behind the wheel, she came rushing back, told the hapless weeping driver to jump into our car, and off we went in hot pursuit of the van. It entered the Hastings Police Thana, off Strand Road and we drove in behind it, racing in so that the driver would not escape into the trees behind. As we followed him into the thana, I was horrified to see, for the very first time in my life, what the inside of a police station looked like.

It was a red and yellow painted single-story building, rather unkempt looking, with shrubs and trees all around. The steps leading up to the front door were worn down the middle, from all the feet that had climbed those stairs. Inside was another story altogether. It was pandemonium. Bang in the middle of the large room was a cage like structure, and inside it a group of disreputable looking people shouting at the top of their voices to be let out. Policemen with *lathis* (batons) were pushing more people into the cage, to contain them. As we entered, the room quietened for a moment, as it registered that a lady and a youngster had appeared in their midst and then with a roar, the commotion restarted with renewed vigour. The criminals behind bars leapt up and down, shaking the bars, yelling obscenities at the cops, as the Officer in Charge of the thana appeared. Ma informed him, to his utter astonishment, that she would like to file a complaint against the police driver for causing an accident. He refused, saying he would not book the driver till he examined our car, insisting that the accident was caused by us because our brakes failed. Realising the fallacy of his argument, since we had not hit the van, he then said that our brakes were too 'strong', causing the crash!

Ma slowly realising the futility of arguing with him, and by now a little nervous in that room full of screaming men, while accompanied by a sniveling driver and a goggle-eyed child, decided to call my uncle who lived close by. The minute she asked to make a call, the OC backed off, asking her who she was about to speak to. He assumed she was going to complain to a senior officer, and he hastily opened a ledger and booked the police driver, smacking him on his head for his carelessness.

We drove off from the thana as soon as we could, dropped the still sniffling driver off near his broken-down car and went home. When we told Baba we had taken a policeman to a thana to book him, at first, he sat with his head in his hands, then he said he would appoint a driver for us, to prevent any further heart attack inducing incidents!

Kites, Rathmela and Pink Sugar Maths

A disadvantage of being born into a Brahmo household was the significant lack of festivities… the Pujos meant very little as far as a religious or even a family celebration went. Instead, we tried to be away for the duration, to avoid the noise and crowded streets by driving off to Ranchi or Hazaribagh, where my paternal aunt had a home.

But the advantage was that as kids we were allowed to celebrate some festivals just for the sheer pleasure of it. Like Rathayatra. My brother and I would collect slivers of bamboo and sheets of glossy 'marble' coloured paper, glue, string, and cast-off wheels of toy cars and put together a 2 or even 3 storied Rath. It would be festooned with triangular flags and paper roses and any other piece of gaily coloured decoration we could find. We were not fully aware of the significance of the festival but reveled in the creative and fun aspect of it.

On the day it started we would tie a long piece of ribbon to the front and carefully wheel it up and down the garden path, giggling at its unroadworthy-ness! It toppled over at the slightest bump so one of us would have to hold it upright!

We begged to go to the Rath mela outside our home, with its stalls selling lovely handcrafted wooden toys, bamboo flutes that never sounded as tuneful when we played them, plastic dolls with painted faces and a whole host of delicious snacks. We were banned from eating the fried stuff, but my ayah would secretly pick up a few pieces of pink and yellow *'math'* (temple shaped sweets made entirely of sugar) which we loved, and hide them in our bedroom for us to eat away from prying eyes!

The other festival I enjoyed was Vishwakarma puja. I loved flying kites and for days before the festival I'd help our cook (an expert) make kites. He would pick up the paraphernalia needed to make them and yards of string for the *'latai'* (spool). Our rooftop, being large enough to run around on, was the ideal place to fly the kites and we'd have spirited fights with neighboring flyers with much jubilation if we 'cut' our opponents and sent their kites off to die!

The Riverside, Picnic Baskets and Warehouses

My paternal grandparents loved going for evening walks. But no outing was ever complete without a picnic basket of goodies, a couple of folding garden chairs and a rug. I would accompany them often when I was young enough not to have too much homework and off we'd go, trundling over the Howrah Bridge which played such an important part in our lives.

It was not as crowded as it is now, though somewhat chaotic with all kinds of cars, buses, lorries and carts going every which way. The only disciplined mode of transport were the trams that kept to their tracks through the center lane of the bridge. One had to be careful not to drive with both wheels on the tram tracks because the car would skid or waver drunkenly out of control and sometimes the wheels would get stuck in the grooves left by trams.

I loved looking up through the rear window at the struts of the bridge passing overhead and the blue sky high above, imagining I was floating in the sky. The river on either side would catch my attention at high tide, when I'd see bits of vegetation floating along and wonder how far the fish below the surface had travelled to come here.

Driving through the hustle and bustle of Burra Bazaar, I'd keep a look out for St Andrews Church coming up ahead in the middle of the road. It looked like a peaceful island in the midst of the chaos of traffic and pedestrians vying for a foothold on pavements crowded with stalls selling all kinds of edibles.

The white clock tower, with the clock face on all four sides, topped by the weather vane pointing up to the sky, the pillars supporting the portico and the surrounding well-kept garden behind the wrought iron fence looked like a place people might want to rest in, take a break from the chaos outside. I imagined an organ playing in the background and candles flickering every time someone opened the doors to let themselves in.

Our destination would not be too far from there, but we would have to pass Dalhousie Square and the Governor's House before turning right towards the river. The huge old trees in the garden and the tall iron gates of the Governor's place looked so grand as though they were guarding a place of great pomp and glory. I'd imagine carriages with white horses driving up to the sweeping marble staircase and ladies in flowing gowns with glittering tiaras and tall men in top hats and long black cloaks alighting from them.

The riverside was enchanting. The evening breeze would make it a pleasant outing. Boats lazily bobbing on the sunlit water. People slowly walking along the path. There were benches to sit on facing the water under big old shade trees. Sometimes we met people my grandparents knew, at other times we'd simply walk from Princep Ghat, past the restaurant built over the water which I think was then called Gay and later Scoop serving delicious ice cream sundaes, to Outram Ghat and back to the car.

Then off to the Ladies Golf Club grounds nestled between the Maidan, the Race Course and Fort William. There we would spread out a *shataranchi* (rug) and unpack the picnic basket. My grandparents would sit comfortably on their folding chairs while I sat on the rug and read a book or simply gazed up at the tall trees and smooth greens around me. As the sky darkened and the crickets began their evening serenade, we would make our way back home.

As we drove down Strand Road, over the slippery cobbled stones, I imagined I was in Dickensian England, where roads were paved with the same black stones, flanked by tall imposing old buildings with a past. I marveled at the enormous Victorian red brick warehouses lining the street on the riverside. They must have seen so much activity during the East India Company's reign, with ships carrying all kinds of cargo docking at the jetties near Kidderpore, unloading their merchandise to have it transported by train, on the tracks running along the river, to the huge warehouses on the Strand.

Cotton, jute, rice, tea and who knows what else must have made their way to these buildings. They had lofty ceilings and multiple iron staircases on the outside, with massive doors and tall windows inside decorative arches. I could picture fusty bespectacled clerks in dark jackets, seated at wooden desks with inkwells and fountain pens busily making entries in large red leather-bound ledgers, keeping track of the day's intake of goods. They would have an air of gravity about them, as they peered frowning over their horn-rimmed glasses perched on beaky noses, making sure that all the merchandise was fully accounted for. The air inside would be dusty, carrying traces of the goods in store, noisy, with the thuds of heavy sacks and boxes landing on the cemented floor. The man heading the group of laborers would be shouting out instructions for the careful unloading and loading of goods. Sadly, by the time I encountered them, the buildings were quiet, the brick facades were crumbling and the huge doors and windows shut, hoping to be made useful once again someday.

As we drove down the street one could see glimpses of the river flowing beyond the warehouses. No longer busy with ships, one could see a few boats and a passenger steamer crossing over to the other side.

Strand Road widened as we approached the Howrah Bridge. To the left below the bridge, one could see the remnants of the flower market in the evening. It was reportedly the largest wholesale flower market in Asia. One had to go really early to get fresh flowers that came in to the city at dawn. You were greeted by heaps of marigolds, long stemmed tuberoses, red pink and yellow roses, gladioli, lilies, chrysanthemums, cockscomb, sunflowers… some made into garlands for the devout, some in wreaths and some strung together as wedding garlands … an endless sea of colour and perfume.

Reed Organs, Magh Utsav and the Indian Flag

Dida had a beautiful reed organ in her living room, that she would play Rabindra sangeet on occasionally. The organ had a lovely deep tone and had to be operated by foot pedals covered in embroidered felt. The organ was regularly cleaned and tuned by a specialist and I'd love watching him open it up to reveal the complex system inside.

When I began playing the piano, I grew to love Baroque composers like Bach and Vivaldi some of whose music was written for the organ and I played some of their sonatas on Dida's instrument. It sounded glorious! I imagined I would eventually become a professional musician someday and tour the world playing for appreciative audiences everywhere. There was just one little drawback! I was terrified of playing in public!

The Calcutta School of Music held annual concerts where its students would play special pieces they had learnt, for an audience consisting of parents and others. Awaiting my turn in the wings, prepped to play, I'd peer through the velvet curtains at the sea of people and I invariably froze in terror. After much persuasion by my teacher, I'd walk shaking in my polished Kowloon shoes and Good Companion's frilly dress to the grand piano on the stage and prepare to play. Not my best moments. Luckily, I don't recall ever fluffing up my piece but it was not an experience I enjoyed. I even played for a notable patron of music, Anthony Lancelot Dias, Former Governor of West Bengal and though there exists somewhere a black and white photo of me at the concert, in a flowered dress with clips in my hair, the memory of my performance remains a blur of nerves.

As for the organ. Dida used to love hearing me play it and one day she said she wanted me to have it, on condition that I perform for her regularly. It was ceremoniously transported to my bedroom which was opposite hers, across the *uthon* and I would play for her every day with my windows wide open so she could hear its beautiful tones. As I grew up and shifted homes it went along with me and I still play on it occasionally, remembering her delighted response.

As a member of a 'practicing Brahmo' family, I was expected to master the art of playing the harmonium and singing Rabindra Sangeet but despite my grandmother's desire that I do so, it never really happened. My Dadu and Dida would celebrate Magh Utsav on the 11th of Magh each year, according to the Bangla calendar, to commemorate the inauguration of the Brahmo Samaj by Raja Ram Mohan Roy. Most years we would attend the prayer service held at one of the Samajes in Calcutta, most often as not, the Sammelan Samaj in Bhowanipore, where the week-long celebrations drew whole families to enjoy the festive air. We looked forward to meeting our cousins and eating the traditional lunch served at the Samaj.

One year Dida and Dadu decided to celebrate Magh Utsav at home. The top floor of our house was built as a large reception room, big enough to seat lots of people. For days before the 11th, the house was in an uproar with frantic preparations for the big day. Cooks were brought in. A temporary kitchen was set up in the courtyard and Dida brought out the massive *dekchis* and *koras* (kitchen utensils) kept in storage for such events.

The reception room was thoroughly cleaned till the floors shone bright and huge colourful *shataranchis* or rugs were laid on the floor, and covered with white sheets. A raised dais was made by Dida's carpenter for the acharya (minister) and the singers to sit on. Flowers came in by the bucketful and were arranged in polished brass vases around the room. The harmonium was taken out of its brass bound wooden box and ceremoniously placed on the dais.

Downstairs, in the *uthon*, one could hear the clatter of long handled *'hatas'* and *'khuntis'* (cooking implements) as the cooks went about the business of making lunch for a hundred people. The best part of the menu were the sweets! Brown *pantuas* (deep fried sweets) glistening in hot sugar syrup, rows and rows of homemade *sandesh* (sweets made of cottage cheese) and huge terracotta hundis of thick sweet *mishti doi*! My bedroom overlooked the courtyard and I clearly remember the amazing aroma of warm *pantuas* swirling around my room as they bobbed up and down in the warm sugar syrup.

The sizzle of *begun bhaja* (fried brinjals), the smell of the special chutney which had dates and raisins in it, made it so difficult to leave and go up to the top floor for the prayer and song ceremony! But clad in our formal clothes, a miniature sari for me and child sized dhoti and kurta for my brother, we had to welcome our guests and help them find a place to sit on the floor. The older invitees were placed in chairs ranged around the sides. The incense sticks had to be replenished and lit, the flowers coming in had to be placed in vases and our cousins had to be shushed into silence as they sat cross legged on the floor. The part solemn- part joyful ceremony over, it was finally lunch time! All us kids were served first in the dining room, being too young to balance plates in our hands or sit comfortably on the floor and not spill our food everywhere.

Another memorable annual event at home was the ceremonial flag hoisting on Independence Day and Republic Day. Dadu had had a permanent flagpole embedded in the top most balcony of our house and we would unfold and hoist the satin flag on these two days. Not content with seeing it flutter high up on the third floor, my brother and I would march around the courtyard with paper flags, imagining that we were keeping time to an invisible drum playing in the background. Though not overtly pushed into being 'patriotic' we were proud to be a part of a country that was independent of outside rulers, and happy to celebrate the events that led up to being free.

I had heard of several members of the extended family being rushed off to far of countries like America for their notoriety and underground work to get rid of our colonial rulers. One of them lived to the age of 102, and rose to fame as an ardent follower of Martin Luther King Junior, taking part in the Selma March alongside him. Another, a close friend of my maternal grandmother, an outspoken freedom fighter undaunted by her femininity, was imprisoned for plotting to bomb the British Governor's car, though she was later released once the sun set on the British Raj in India.

Christmas Cake, Ham and a Tree

One holiday and festival we really looked forward to was Christmas. Firstly, being in a school run by Irish Missionaries, the whole idea of celebrating Christmas was ingrained in us as a time for exchanging presents, wishing everyone and feasting on goodies. The weather grew pleasant, winter clothes made their appearance, we changed into our darker uniforms for school, stockings made their way into our wardrobes and preparations for the big day began at home.

My mom would bake an enormous fruit cake filled with currants, candied fruits, walnuts, almonds and cherries. We were given the task of chopping these into small pieces, some of which of course we popped into our mouths when Ma wasn't looking. After baking the cake, well in advance of D-day, it would be periodically treated to a few ounces of brandy, spooned into tiny holes drilled into the body of the cake. Then came the almond icing or marzipan. Once wholly covered, the leftover icing would be shaped into flowers and used to decorate the top.

The other big ritual was the whole leg of ham roasted with a liberal glazing of honey, dotted with whole cloves and scored in a crisscrossed pattern. The gas oven would be fired up and heated in advance while preparing the ham, as it was trussed up with twine and placed in a metal tray with inch high sides. Basting the ham was Ma's domain as the oven was too hot for us to use safely, and the kitchen would fill with the aromas of butter and honey on the glowing ham every time she opened the oven door. The basting liquid would be made into a beautiful sauce and poured into a pretty sauce boat.

Putting up the tree meant pulling out all the decorations stored away, to which we added new bits and pieces every year. My favourites were the shiny glass balls and stars. Being the youngest in the house I'd have the honour of placing the angel on top, and I was hoisted up to reach the pinnacle. We made paper icicles by folding sheets of paper into a triangular shape and cutting out bits to create the design. Smaller ones were hung on the tree, larger icicles were used as table decoration.

Red and white candles in decorative candleholders, placed on a white lace tablecloth, the 'good' China with its intricate floral border in gold and russet, red napkins in napkin rings and wine and water glasses were set up before our guests arrived. I would be put in charge of creating the flower arrangements for the dining table, sideboard and living room. Roses and baby's breath were my flowers of choice for the dining table, in a round glass vase.

In those days, the house was often filled with music of some sort. When it was just the family, the strains of Bach's Violin concertos or Beethoven's thunderous symphonies would fill the rooms downstairs. Depending on the occasion, the music would change to foot stomping jazz or rock and roll, and quite a few enthusiastic dancers would dance the evening away. Christmas meant carols to begin with, or the melodious voices of people like Nana Mouskouri and Aretha Franklin. We were allowed to stay up beyond our rigidly followed bedtime to enjoy the festivities with the other kids visiting our home.

Teatime, Bottlebrush and a Cycle

Sunday mornings I woke up to the trundle of the lawn mower making its way across the garden. Its rollers made a clackety clack sound as it trimmed the grass, freshly cut pieces of which would leap into the green metallic basket attached to the side. As it moved from one end of the garden to the other, I could hear the excited chirps of sparrows as the mower exposed a few earthworms and other delicacies that the birds would quickly gobble up before the mower made its way back.

Time for me to quickly get ready to tend to the garden under Dida's watchful eye. She would be sitting on a white cane chair with a tea table next to her, a white frilly sunshade attached to the back to protect her delicate skin. A flowered tea pot covered with a crisp white cosy embroidered with tiny flowers, a matching tea cup and saucer, sugar bowl and milk jug within easy reach sat on the table. A flowered plate resting on a lace doily with a couple of Marie biscuits completed the picture.

After a hug I'd be given my instructions. 'Use the *khurpi* (gardening trowel) to dig up the weeds from the flower beds. This was something I loved. I felt important… no weed would be allowed to ruin Dida's garden. Despite the mud under my fingernails, I'd happily crouch down and dig out the offending plants, and toss them into the small *jhuri* (wicker basket) I carried with me. Nasturtiums, sun flowers, larkspurs, petunia, and of course roses bloomed at different times of the year. Easter lilies and flowering cacti made special appearances.

The bottle brush tree drooped over the lawn, jasmine bushes added a delicate aroma at one end of the garden, the powerful perfume of the *Champa* wound its way into your senses at the other end. The beautiful milky white magnolia blossoms swayed on the branches of the tree on one corner of the garden next to the *Raat ki Rani* which only bloomed in the quiet of the night.

The garden was my place of retreat. Under the bottlebrush tree with its drooping red flowers, I'd place a couple of cushions, my books, crayons, drawing book and the favourite toy of the day and if I was lucky, a snack or two. Ginger biscuits with their oddly zingy crunch, or Nahoum's macaroons with their sweet coconut centers. A hot day meant either ice cream soda or chilled ginger ale. Sometimes my brother joined me with a book or two and afternoons would pass in companionable silence.

The garden was edged with a walkway tiled with pale yellow pink and white slabs. Many games of hopscotch and marbles later, it became my cycling path. Afternoons after school I'd cycle up our driveway across the path and down my Dida's driveway merrily ringing my bell to announce my presence.

One day, as I cycled up and down the path, completing my rounds by turning on to the driveways that formed the arms of the U of my cycling route, I forgot to ring my bell and I came head-to-head with my Uncle's Jeep. He had driven it out of the garage at the back and was heading towards the gate when I banged into his fender that sent me skidding along the wall, and under the Jeep! He had come to a complete halt upon seeing me, but as I disappeared under him, he went into shock, believing he'd run me over!

As it happened, my leg had caught in the chain, which got embedded in my shin, and my arm had scraped along the wall as I skidded, but I was very much alive and screeching like a banshee! Various members of the household came running hearing the commotion, and hauled me out along with the mangled bike. The frame was bent out of shape and so was I! Liberal amounts of Dettol and hugs later I was severely admonished for my carelessness. I think my uncle forgot all about going out and retired to his room to recuperate!

Apart from the flowers and plants, the garden hid quite a lot of treasures. Snails made their somewhat slimy way across the lawn, frogs leapt about in glee through the monsoons, crickets rubbed their legs undaunted by my threats to be silent, and birds… so many different birds alighted in this oasis in the middle of a busy city. Perhaps the greenery caught their eye as they flew high above and they came to investigate or perhaps take a break from their summer or winter migrations.

Besides the raucous *shalik* (mynah) and the sparrows and crows, we often saw bright green parrots on the fruit trees. Kingfishers, owls with their yellow unblinking eyes and fluffy chests, woodpeckers, tiny fluttering hummingbirds and a few unidentified visitors made our garden their temporary residence. The pigeons were another story. Perhaps being urban birds, they preferred to roost on parts of the house rather than the garden, making quite a mess in the process. Much to our horror, one particularly lush bougainvillea became the home of a band of bees. The threat of getting stung kept us at a distance but the gardener smoked them away and we enjoyed fresh home-grown honey on scones and pancakes.

I would often sit on the sun warmed steps leading down to the garden, at dusk, playing my recorder, or at times the bright green and white melodica, the odd cross between a piano and a wind instrument. Perhaps that is what kept the mosquitos away!

Glossary

aamsatta bricks (layers of sundried sweet mango pulp)
aloo dum (potato curry)
anchal (end of a sari)
begun (brinjals)
bhajas (fritters)
bhandar ghor (store room for household items
boams (ceramic mason jars)
boris (sundried lentil dumplings)
boti (Bengali kitchen knife)
chaklas (discs)
chorchori (mixed vegetable curry)
dalan (courtyard)
dhabas (roadside eateries)
Dida & Dadu (paternal grandmother and grandfather)
Didama & Dadu (maternal grandmother and grandfather)
dimer dalna (egg curry)
gamlas (basins)
gandharaj lebu (aromatic lemon)
ganney ki ras (fresh sugarcane juice)
haldi (turmeric)
hatas and *khuntis* (cooking implements)
jeebeygoja (sugar coated pastry)
jhuris (wicker baskets)
jhurjhure (finely cut)
kamranga (star fruit)
kalojeerey (black cumin)
karelas (bitter gourd)
Kashphool (wild grass)
kharams (wooden clogs)
koyla ghar (coal room)

kuler achaar (Indian plum pickle)
kulos (wicker trays)
kurkurey aloo bhaja, (potato crisps)
kutno (cutting, slicing, dicing vegetables, fish, poultry and meat)
lassi (drink made with curd)
latai (spool)
luchis (fried flatbread)
mali (gardener)
mishti doi (sweet yogurt)
mocha (banana flower)
nankhatai biscuits (shortbread biscuits)
nimkis (savory snacks)
panchphoron (5 spices)
panchrang achaar (five spice pickle)
pantuas (deep fried sweets)
patishaptas (sweet crepes)
pidi (low wooden stool)
Pishima (father's sister)
Rajbaris (royal mansions)
sandesh (sweets made of cottage cheese)
shalik (mynah)
shataranchi (rug)
tapari (cape gooseberry)
thalas (plates)
thor (heart of a banana tree trunk)
tokri (basket)
tonga (horse carriage)
ucchey (bitter gourd)
uthon (courtyard)

www.ingramcontent.com/pod-product-compliance
Ingram Content Group UK Ltd
Pitfield, Milton Keynes, MK11 3LW, UK
UKRC031637240426
12048UKWH00035B/92